BAPTISM IN THE
EARLY CHURCH

BAPTISM IN THE EARLY CHURCH

by

PROF. H.F. STANDER
&
PROF. J.P. LOUW

Carey Publications

A Carey Press title
published by Reformation Today Trust
in cooperation with
The Association of Reformed Baptist Churches of America.

© REFORMATION TODAY TRUST 2004. 75 Woodhill Road, Leeds, LS16 7BZ, England. All rights reserved. No part of this publication may be reproduced, stored in a retrieval system or transmitted, in any form, or by any means, electronic, mechanical, photocopying, recording or otherwise, without the prior permission of the publishers.

ISBN 0 9527913 1 5

Distributed by
EVANGELICAL PRESS
Faverdale North Industrial Estate, Darlington, DL3 0PH, England

Evangelical Press USA
P. O. Box 825, Webster, New York 14580, USA
e-mail: sales@evangelicalpress.org
web: http://www.evangelicalpress.org

Unless otherwise indicated, Scripture quotations in this publication are from the Holy Bible, New International Version. Copyright © 1973, 1978, 1984, International Bible Society. Used by permission of Hodder & Stoughton, a member of the Hodder Headline Group. All rights reserved.

Printed and bound in the United States of America.

First published in 1988 and 1994 (revised edition)
By Didaskalia Publishers, South Africa.

Contents

	PAGE
Foreword by J.M. Renihan	7
Preface	13
1. Baptism and the use of church history by modern scholars	15
2. The Apostolic Fathers (1st/2nd century)	31
3. Aristides of Athens (2nd century)	43
4. Justin (100-165)	46
5. Irenaeus (140/160-(?)200)	51
6. Clement of Alexandria (150-215)	56
7. Tertullian (c. 160-220)	63
8. Hippolytus (170-236)	73
9. Origen (185-254) (185-254)	81
10. Christian tomb inscriptions	91
11. *Didascalia Apostolorum* (3rd century)	96
12. Novatian (190/210-257/8)	102
13. Cyprian (200/210-257)	105
14. Eusebius (263-339/40)	117
15. Cyril of Jerusalem (315-386)	120
16. Asterius the Sophist (4th century)	125
17. Basil the Great (330-379)	130
18. Gregory of Nazianzus (330-389)	133
19. Gregory of Nyssa (335-394)	141
20. Ambrose (339-397)	143
21. Apostolic Constitutions (380)	154
22. Etheria (381/384)	157
23. Chrysostom (350-407)	162
24. Theodore of Mopsuestia (350-428)	169
25. Early Christian art	172
26. Conclusions	180
Bibliography	187

Foreword

James M. Renihan

In theological debate, history should never be the final judge; that place is reserved for Scripture. History may, however, make a significant contribution to the discussion, shedding light on the practices of those living closest to the era of the Bible. In the debate over the subjects of baptism, historiography has had a long and fascinating part to play in determining the conclusions of many.

From the first appearance of English churches practising believer's baptism by immersion in the 1640s until today, attempts have been made to investigate and present conclusions about the practice of baptism in the early church. Several efforts were made in the seventeenth century, the most notable and successful of them being Henry D'Anvers' 1673 work entitled *A Treatise of Baptism*, followed by a second revised and enlarged edition in 1674.[1] This remarkable work of almost 450 pages was something of a *tour de force* for its age, and has been regarded as such since then. William Cathcart wrote of this *Treatise*, it 'was the ablest on the subject published by any Baptist till that time' while J.M. Cramp said that Danvers' book was 'regarded as the most learned and complete work which at

---

[1] Henry Danvers, *A Treatise of Baptism: Wherein, that of Believers, and that of Infants, is examined by the Scriptures*. The second edition with large additions. (London: Printed for Fran. Smith, at the Elephant and Castle near the Royal Exchange in Cornhil, 1674).

that time had been published on the subject'.² In the book, D'Anvers sought to demonstrate from Scripture and history that believer's baptism was the practice of the apostolic era. So convincing was the work that several paedobaptist authors, including Richard Baxter, entered the lists in opposition, seeking to staunch the bleeding as people flocked to join the Baptist churches.

Since D'Anvers' day, many other excursions into the literature of the early Christian centuries have come from the presses. As recently as the 1960s, Joachim Jeremias and Kurt Aland engaged in a spirited printed debate over the question. As one might expect, in almost every case during this time period, the authors have published their conclusions as polemics for their particular view. Paedobaptists argue that the early church practised infant baptism; Baptists argue that it did not.

Frequently paedobaptist authors are heard to claim that the unanimous historical testimony of the ancient church is in favour of infant baptism, and that the believer's baptism view is a relatively recent development, and thus illegitimate. Such a notion is not new, it has been promoted for years. The confluence of new and old may be noted in the recent reprint of George W. Bethune's lectures on the Heidelberg Catechism, entitled *Guilt, Grace and Gratitude*.³ Bethune states quite directly,

> Our church ... requires that the *infant offspring* of believers should also be baptized. This we hold in common with all Christians who practised baptism until comparatively modern times, and with the vast majority of Christians

---

²William Cathcart, *The Baptist Encyclopedia*, (Paris, Ark.: The Baptist Standard Bearer, 1988 reprint of 1881 edition), s.v. 'D'Anvers, Gov. Henry'; J.M. Cramp, *Baptist History*, (Watertown, Wis.: Baptist Heritage Publications, 1987 reprint of 1871 edition), 373.
³George W. Bethune, *Guilt, Grace and Gratitude: Lectures on the Heidelberg Catechism* (Edinburgh: The Banner of Truth Trust, 2001 reprint of 1864 edition).

now. The usage of infant baptism may be distinctly traced in Christian writers from the close of the apostolic age all the way down... Here, then, we have the opinion of the whole Christian world from the apostolic age, both before and after the reformation, – the Baptists excepted... Our opponents cannot show us the slightest evidence that the practice was introduced at any time, though, had it been an innovation, it would have been noted, and would have caused discussion. The utter absence of all proof, or even surmise to the contrary, indicates that it has come to us from the apostles themselves.[4]

This language is not atypical. It is repeated regularly in contemporary literature and sermonic presentations. For these men, the matter has been settled, in favour of paedobaptism. If this is true, it is a powerful support for the defence of that position.

The present work is another foray into this historical battlefield. One might question its importance and validity – is it simply another attempt at polemics, interpreting the primary source documents from a denominational perspective? Herein is its value. The authors, two internationally known and highly regarded classical scholars, members of paedobaptist churches, present a dispassionate examination of the problem, based on a careful treatment of primary sources. They approach the issue from their area of specialty and expertise, through the discipline of classical historiography, not denominational polemics, and produce a work singularly authoritative.

While the reader must determine for himself the strength of the argument presented, one must acknowledge the unique credibility attached to the work. Had it been penned by authors with Baptist convictions, it might be dismissed as an instance of denominational polemics (although it would still deserve

---

[4]Bethune, 2:245-49, emphasis his.

careful evaluation). Since these men have no such party axes to grind, their conclusions deserve serious attention.

Essentially, they argue that infant baptism was *not* the practice of the Apostles and their immediate successors, but developed through the convergence of several factors. Gradually, paedobaptism came to be the majority position in the church, but probably not until the latter part of the fourth century. Such conclusions directly contradict the assertions of George Bethune cited above, and stand as a significant challenge to paedobaptist apologists. If the primary source material demonstrates that infant baptism is the result of such development, its defenders ought to take a long second look at the Scriptures, examining them for confirmation of their doctrine. We have said that history is not determinative, but in this case it is an important primary witness, and must not be ignored.

This is a helpful book. It demonstrates that believer's baptism did not simply disappear after the apostolic era, but continued to be the accepted position for centuries. Infant baptism became part of ecclesiastical practice gradually, apart from apostolic injunction. For this reason, it must be called into question, and rejected as a suitable practice for Christian churches.

A few words about the book are in order. It was written in the context of theological discussion in South Africa, and thus primarily reflects the literature circulating in that country. Those familiar with the discussion will recognize that the issues presented are not different from those circulated in Europe or North America. It is hoped that the reader in the West will be familiar with these arguments, and be able to supply the necessary references. The authors have chosen to employ a somewhat unusual reference system, minimizing footnotes and bringing bibliographic material more directly into the text. It has been thought unnecessary to alter this system, as it is fairly straightforward and will not hinder the reader from consulting the sources cited. A few minor editorial changes have been made to the work with the permission of the authors, seeking to make it conform more closely to a familiar style.

May the Lord use this book to bring continued reformation to the churches.

James M. Renihan
2004

Preface

In this work the Greek, Latin and Syrian sources on the practice of baptism in the first four centuries are studied. It is not the aim of the authors to promote any theological point of view, but rather to make the ancient writings on this subject accessible to the English reader in an objective way. The writings of this era are important since they reveal the origins and developments of Christian practices and dogmas.

The target group is both scholars and ordinary believers who want to know from where traditions stem.

The Authors
Department of Ancient Languages
University of Pretoria
0002 PRETORIA
South Africa

CHAPTER 1

Baptism and the use of church history by modern scholars

In the history of the Christian churches the rite of baptism has been a contentious issue for many centuries. In our time, and especially during the past decades, baptism has become a hotly debated issue. The central questions in this debate are concerned with the recipients of the act of baptism (infants or believers) and the mode of baptism (sprinkling or immersion). These two main themes lead to other questions concerning the covenant (especially the Abrahamic covenant and circumcision), and also eventual rebaptism.

Debaters, irrespective of whatever point of view they support, are naturally convinced that their interpretation of baptism is indeed scriptural. Moreover, it has also become very common in this debate to appeal to the history of the early church.[1] Scholars are often led by their theological presuppositions when they claim that history supports their particular point of view. All the different perspectives concerning baptism have been 'proved' by quotations from the writers of the early church. Consequently, people today have a very perplexed picture of the practice of baptism in the early church. This might

---

[1] The term 'early church' has become conventionalized and is used as such in this book. However, the reader is advised to bear in mind that in reality there was no unified church during the first centuries but numerous Christian congregations, and often regional groupings. The term 'early church' should be understood as a cover term for all the Christian communities.

lead people to conclude that the early Christians were very much confused. The truth is that modern day authors misinterpret and sometimes misrepresent the statements of the Church Fathers.

It is not the aim of this book to defend any theological point of view. Certainly not. The purpose of this study is to present the information about the actual rite of baptism in the writings of the early church as literally as possible, and in historical order, so as to provide a source book which may be of help to debaters in their quest for the practice of baptism in the first four centuries A.D. We also include such sources as tombstone inscriptions and early Christian art. The contention of this book will rather be to let the Church Fathers speak for themselves on this issue. Naturally, a specific quotation cannot be fully appreciated unless it is understood within the total context in which it appears, and with due attention to the requirements of the linguistic and literary features of significance in reading a text. Such comments will accompany the quotations in order to furnish the reader with the necessary background information required to appreciate the referential meaning(s) of the quotations. In several instances comments by modern authors on specific passages will also be discussed to illustrate how particular passages were interpreted by various debaters. However, before one can seriously expound the Patristic sources, the methodology of this study has to be related to many other studies of the history of the rite of baptism prevalent in the writings of various debaters. In order to underscore the need for an objective and scientific presentation of baptism in the early church, a survey will now be given of some of the statements occurring frequently in modern literature. It will clearly illustrate how scholars (mis)represent church history.

One of the most striking aspects of the arguments proposed by supporters of infant baptism, is that they are not content to accept that the inception of the baptism of infants occurred at some time and place in the history of the early church, but that they are usually very keen to find proof – even if it is only indirect - of a *common* practice right from the time of the New Testament onwards. Apart from a few, such as Kurt Aland (1963), the general procedure is to argue for their theological position on the basis of possibilities, without weighing the complete data, in order to evaluate the actual state of affairs in the early church. A typical example is the extensively documented work by Joachim Jeremias (1960). The concern is primarily whether infant baptism did occur, not what facts are available on baptism. Jeremias quotes forty ancient documents as sources, of which twenty five are designated as explicit references to infant baptism – the earliest dating from 200 A.D., namely, Tertullian's treatise called *On Baptism* (*De Baptismo*). Tertullian lived at a time when quite contrary views on baptism were prevalent, viz. that it should be administered as close as possible to death, since baptism was regarded as cleansing a person from all sin (and thus affording less opportunity to sin again). Others advocated an early baptism to remove inherited sin. Tertullian disapproved of both practices. In the *On Baptism* he criticized the baptism of *parvuli*, that is, small children. He, as a lawyer, was very much concerned about a person's responsibility in making decisions, and therefore advocated that children should be baptized when they could be taught and could understand what it required to be a Christian.

Many scholars refer to the above-mentioned passage in Tertullian as clear evidence of infant baptism in the early church (*The Oxford Dictionary of the Christian Church* 1978:701; *The Westminster Dictionary of Church History* 1971:83; Pitchers in König 1984:32). The passage in Tertullian runs as follows:

> And so, according to the circumstances and disposition, and even age, of each individual, the delay of baptism is preferable; principally, however, in the case of little children. For why is it necessary – if (baptism itself) is not so necessary – that the sponsors likewise should be thrust into danger? Who both themselves, by reason of mortality, may fail to fulfil their promises, and may be disappointed

by the development of an evil disposition, in those for whom they stood? The Lord does indeed say, 'Forbid them not to come unto me'. Let them 'come,' then, while they are growing up; let them 'come' while they are learning, while they are learning whither to come; let them become Christians when they have become able to know Christ. Why does the innocent period of life hasten to the 'remission of sins?' More caution will be exercised in worldly matters: so that one who is not trusted with earthly substance is trusted with divine! (Tertullian *On Baptism* 18)

This passage from Tertullian is indeed the earliest reference in early Christian writings to children being baptized. However, to equate the baptism of children with the baptism of babies, as adherents of infant baptism prefer to do, is to neglect the fact that these children were not baptized within a theological framework of the Abrahamic covenant and circumcision. The passage from Tertullian does not speak of infant baptism as it is understood today; it merely refers to a practice among some Christians (of which Tertullian disapproves) to baptize people at a very early stage as small children. It is also remarkable that Tertullian refers to sponsors who probably had to go through the ceremony on behalf of these little ones. This was done at a time (which will be discussed in subsequent chapters of this book) when baptism was regarded as one's guarantee to enter the Kingdom of heaven. As a safeguard, in order to avoid the possibility of little ones dying before they are grown and able to partake of the ritual themselves, sponsors substituted on their behalf. That is why Tertullian advises that such baptisms are undesirable and should be postponed until the recipients can understand what is actually at stake.

It is important to account for the meaning as well as procedures of baptism in the early stages of the Christian church before one can compare ancient and modern practices. This is exactly what Jeremias (1960:98) suggested at the very end of his book without elaborating on this extremely important issue. Perhaps we should herein see the reason why Jeremias has become an important reference book for supporters of infant baptism though he actually only talked about the baptism of children. However, even Aland (1963) understood him as defending infant baptism, and as such he criticises a number of the assumptions made by Jeremias. Many others have since used the data as applying to infant baptism though in the vast majority of the 'clear' cases quoted by Jeremias the issue was children, not specifically babies. This distinction is hardly ever made in the debate.

It is remarkable that though there are a number of references in ancient sources to the baptism of children, these are perhaps of too late a date to have gained much attention. The general tendency seems to seek proof of infant baptism in documents much closer to the time of the New Testament even though these may be 'indirect'.

A.C. Barnard gives the following as an 'indirect proof' of infant baptism in the early church:

Justin Martyr writes in his first Apology ± 165: "There are among us many, both men and women, who have been Christ's disciples from childhood, and who remain pure at the age of sixty or seventy years."

Barnard then concludes:

This refers to the time when they received their status of discipleship, i.e. at their baptism. Thus they must have been baptized ± 80-90 A.D.[2]

---

[2] The original Afrikaans version reads as follows:
Justinus die Martelaar skryf in sy eerste Apologie ± 165: 'Daar is by ons baie sestig- en sewentigjarige manne en vroue wat van kindsbeen af Christene was en steeds onbedorwe gebly het.' Dit wys op die tyd toe hulle die status van dissipelskap ontvang het, d.w.s. by die doop. Hulle moes dan hulle doop ± 80-90 n.C. ontvang het. (Barnard 1984:78)

But when Justin says that someone has been a Christian from childhood, that surely would not imply that such a person was indeed baptized, specifically as an infant. The phrase 'from childhood' – in the Greek ἐκ παίδων (*Apology* I,15,6) – refers to the early years of a person's life. It may extend up to the age of puberty and somewhat beyond. Regularly in the ancient world persons were referred to as children up to about 16–18 years of age. This allows for a much wider extent of time than the few weeks since birth, presently associated with the age of a youngster being baptized as an infant. As we will see later on in this study, children who confessed that they believed in the Father, the Son and the Holy Spirit, were occasionally baptized. It was not the age that qualified a person for baptism, but confession of belief. Therefore, one can only say from Justin's remark that the people referred to had probably been baptized during the early years of their life. One still has to show what this rite of baptism entailed, and also how old they were at the time.

For this reason the reference quoted by Barnard as a possibility of infant baptism in the early church is not only unconvincing, but Barnard also fails to tell his readers that there are a number of explicit descriptions of the nature of baptism, namely believer's baptism, in this same work of Justin, from which he has taken the above-mentioned quotation. The following excerpt will suffice:

> As many as are persuaded and believe that what we teach and say is true, and undertake to be able to live accordingly, are instructed to pray and to entreat God with fasting, for the remission of their sins that are past, we praying and fasting with them. Then they are brought by us where there is water, and are regenerated in the same manner in which we were ourselves regenerated. For, in the name of God, the Father and Lord of the universe, and of our Saviour Jesus Christ, and of the Holy

Spirit, they then receive the washing with water. (Justin *Apology* I,61)

One may speculate why Barnard resorts to an 'indirect proof' of infant baptism in Justin's *Apology* but ignores a 'direct proof' of believer's baptism in the same work!

W. Oetting argues on even less convincing grounds as follows:

> It should be noted, however, that neither Justin Martyr nor the *Didache* mentions infant baptism. The literature seems to assume it, just as the New Testament apparently does. (Oetting 1970:31)

Oetting is employing here a rather haphazard form of argumentation based on the fact that if a matter was not recorded in a writing, one can assume that it is taken for granted. But one is on very shaky ground when one argues that an author is actually giving his tacit approval of infant baptism, or any other issue for that matter, when he does not mention it in his work. If this form of argumentation were allowed, one might as well argue that because rebaptism, or even the baptism of non-human beings for that matter, is not mentioned, 'the literature seems to assume it'. Oetting, too, prefers not to mention the explicit references to believer's baptism in Justin's writings.

As is evident in the quotation above, Oetting also refers to the *Didache* as a work which 'seems to assume' infant baptism though it does not mention it. When we look at the *Didache*, however, we read the following:

> But before baptism let the baptizer fast, and the one baptized, and whatever others can; but you should order the baptized to fast one or two days before. (*The Didache* 7,4)

It is unclear how one can conclude from this work that the author 'seems to assume' infant baptism. The pre-baptismal fasting would rather *not* suggest that infants are involved. This is also the conclusion of Engelbrecht, though he stands in the tradition of infant baptism, when he remarks:

> Justin and the Didache contain no reference whatsoever to infant baptism ...[3]

W. Marais, however, a proponent of infant baptism, does not want to concede this and really presses the text when he says:

> I find nothing in this passage which teaches that the baptismal candidate should be an adult, since an infant, too, can fast.[4]

In order to 'prove' that infants can fast, he refers to Jonah 3:5-8[5] and Joel 2:15-16.[6] However, these two passages are not

---

[3] The original Afrikaans versions reads as follows:
Justinus en die *Didache* verwys hoegenaamd nie na die kinderdoop nie ....
(Engelbrecht 1984:57)

[4] The original Afrikaans versions reads as follows:
Ek vind in hierdie gedeelte niks wat leer dat die dopeling 'n volwassene moet wees nie, want ook 'n suigeling kan vas. (Marais 1974:143)

[5] Jonah 3:5-8 reads as follows: 'The Ninevites believed God. They declared a fast, and all of them, from the greatest to the least, put on sackcloth. When the news reached the king of Nineveh, he rose from his throne, took off his royal robes, covered himself with sackcloth and sat down in the dust. Then he issued a proclamation in Nineveh: "By the decree of the king and his nobles: Do not let any man or beast, herd or flock, taste anything; do not let them eat or drink. But let man and beast be covered with sackcloth. Let everyone call urgently on God. Let them give up their evil ways and their violence...."'

[6] Joel 2:15-16 reads as follows: 'Blow the trumpet in Zion, declare a holy fast, call a sacred assembly. Gather the people, consecrate the assembly; bring together the elders, gather the children, those nursing at the breast. Let the bridegroom leave his room and the bride her chamber.'

applicable since we have a number of specific references in the literature of the early church where the pre-baptismal period is described as a time of devotion, instruction, prayer and fasting. As a matter of fact, fasting regularly involved devotion, prayer and even instruction (see, for example, Justin *Apology* I,61 quoted above). What is more, it is not the mere *ability* to abstain from food that is at stake, but rather the *devotional preparation* that is required. The circumstances referred to in Jonah and Joel are quite remote from that of the *Didache*. If one were to insist on equating these passages itemwise, one would have to allow for animals to be baptized since in the Jonah passage even animals were required to fast. No one, however, would want to go that far. Finally, one does not need Jonah or Joel to argue as Marais does. Common sense allows for babies to be able to fast. But, once again, it is not a question of what is remotely possible, but what the early texts at large seem to suggest. An argument based on a remote assumption, as Marais proposed, is hardly an adequate way of dealing with the subject. If the *Didache* requires fasting as a pre-baptismal event, one has to inquire into the nature of the fasting merely abstaining from food, or are there other events involved.

Barnard gives three more examples of, what he believes, are indirect proof of infant baptism. He states as follows:

> He (Polycarp) was bishop of Smyrna and he died on 22 February 156. Before he died as a martyr, he was asked by Statius Quadratus to revile Christ. Polycarp then answered: "For eighty six years have I been his servant, and he has done me no wrong, and how can I blaspheme my King who saved me?" (*Martyrdom of Polycarp* 9,3).[7]

---

[7] The original Afrikaans version reads as follows:
Hy (Polycarpus) was biskop van Smirna en sterf 22 Februarie 156. Voor hy die marteldood sterf word hy deur Statius Quadratus gevra om Christus te vervloek. Hierop antwoord hy: 'Ses en tagtig jaar dien ek Hom en Hy het my nooit enige kwaad aangedoen nie, hoe sou ek my Koning kon laster wat my verlos het' (*Martyrium Polycarpi* 9,3). (Barnard 1984:78)

Barnard maintains that the age of Polycarp proves that he was probably born in the year A.D. 70 and that he was baptized as an infant. His opinion concerning this quotation is shared by the *Oxford Dictionary of the Christian Church* (1978: 701) and Wand (1949:96). It is nevertheless unclear how one can conclude from this passage that if Polycarp was baptized in the year A.D.70, he must have been a baby at that time. The *Martyrdom of Polycarp* (*Martyrium Polycarpi*) does not say that he was baptized as an infant, it merely says that he had been a Christian for 86 years. Polycarp could have been baptized as a young person and still referred to his service to the Lord as a period of 86 years. How can we be sure that he was not 90 years or more of age when he suffered martyrdom? Moreover, he even could have been 86 years and was merely referring to his 'whole life' as a speech act without exactly counting the days one by one.

Note also the following remark by Barnard:

> Polycrates, bishop of Ephesus ± 190/91. He states that seven members of his family were bishops and that he himself was the eighth. 'I, your brother, lived for 65 years in the Lord.' This shows that he must have been baptized as a child in ± 125.[8]

Again, there is no proof at all that the 65 years were counted precisely from a few weeks after he had been born. The 65 years merely refers to his life as a believer. It does not state when he became a believer.

Barnard (and Jeremias 1958:63ff.) also refer to the letter of Pliny, which was written in 111/112 A.D., as an indirect proof of infant baptism:

---

[8] The original Afrikaans version reads as follows:
Polycrates, biskop van Efese ± 190/91. Hy vermeld dat sewe van sy familielede biskoppe was en hy self die agtste. 'Ek, julle broer, het 65 jaar in die Here geleef.' Dit wys daarop dat hy reeds as kind in ± 125 gedoop moes gewees het. (Barnard 1984:78)

The letter of Pliny to Caesar Trajan, dated 111/112. In this letter it is stated that the congregation consists of children ('teneri') as well as older people ('robustiores') who had come from paganism to the Christian Church.[9]

But let us put this letter in its context: Pliny was the governor of Bithynia when he wrote the above-mentioned letter to Trajan. This letter describes the pursuit and execution of Christians in Pliny's province. In it Pliny asks Trajan, amongst other things, whether he should sentence only those Christians who are proved to be criminals, or everybody who calls himself a Christian. He also asks if he should pardon apostates. In this context, then, Pliny says:

> Nor am I at all sure whether any distinction should be made between them on the grounds of age, or if young people ('teneri') and adults ('robustiores') should be treated alike. (*The Letters of Pliny* xcvi,2)

This text definitely does not tell us anything about *babies* being baptized. As a matter of fact, the content clearly speaks about believers who had to stand trial because of their faith in Jesus. It seems more reasonable to conclude from this passage that these 'teneri' had confessed their faith in Jesus, which obviously excludes babies. Moreover, the Latin term *teneri* (in conjunction with *robustiores*) probably designates young people (in contrast with older people) though *teneri* in Latin generally refers to young children. Even if it referred to infants, however, the issue is not baptism, but who of the Christian community should be punished.

---

[9] The original Afrikaans version reads as follows:
Die brief van Plinius aan keiser Trajanus, gedateer 111/112. Hierin word vermeld dat die gemeente bestaan uit kinders ('teneri'), naas oueres ('robustiores') wat uit die heidendom tot die Christelike kerk toegetree het. (Barnard 1984:79)

At this stage one should observe that the examples quoted to substantiate instances of infant baptism are all of a secondary nature in that they are remote possibilities, if indeed they are possibilities at all. This is surely not a scientific procedure for the investigation of a given situation. One should rather collect all *real*, that is, *explicit* references to baptism and examine all the data. Only then can one consider such rather vague instances, in the light of the entire picture. It is therefore clear that the authors were not concerned with investigating the data as such - they had a given conviction and were groping for 'proofs'.

Another example of a misrepresentation of church history can be found in the following statement of L.J.C. Van den Berg:

> The early Church Fathers saw baptism as an initiation rite into participating in the church ... Infant baptism was already valid in the time of Origen and Tertullian. The general belief was that nobody could be rebaptized if he had already been baptized in the name of the Father and the Son and the Holy Spirit.[10]

It is not true that the conviction among many Church Fathers was that a person who had been baptized in the name of the Father and of the Son and of the Holy Ghost should not be baptized again. It would be more correct to say that there was a heated discussion in the early church concerning rebaptism. There was no uniform decision and different opinions prevailed in different regions. (See the *Oxford Dictionary of the Christian Church* 1978:127). But Van den Berg is making an even more serious mistake when he fails to tell his readers that

---

[10] The original Afrikaans version reads as follows:
Die vroeë kerkvaders het die doop as 'n unisiasie (sic) rite (sic) tot deelname aan die kerk gesien ... Suigeling doop (sic) was alreeds in die tyd van Origenes en Tertullianus geldig. Die algemene opvatting was dat daar geensins 'n herdoop (wederdoop) kon plaasvind as die persoon alreeds in die naam van die Vader en die Seun en die Heilige Gees gedoop is nie. (Van den Berg 1981:26)

the early church used the term 'rebaptism' in a completely different sense than that in which it is used today. The term 'rebaptism' is used today when someone dissociates himself from his baptism as an infant and then requests to be baptized anew. Van den Berg apparently uses the term 'rebaptism' in this sense in the above-mentioned quotation since it is linked with a statement regarding infant baptism. In the early church, however, the term 'rebaptism' was used when someone went over from a heretical group to the orthodox church and asked to be baptized again. The Church Fathers then debated the validity of baptisms which were administered outside the orthodox church. Thus it was never a matter of rebaptizing someone who had presumably undergone infant baptism, but rebaptizing a person who had been baptized in an unorthodox group. Thus Van den Berg has to distinguish between the 'rebaptism' of the early church and the 'rebaptism' of the modern church.

The above examples are but a few illustrating how easily texts are haphazardly offered as proofs. We may also note that often general claims are made without explicit quotations, but merely references to authors' views on baptism. Tertullian is again a favourite in this respect. The following serves as a good example of this type of claim:

Barnard claims that in another work of Tertullian the latter pleads for infant baptism as being an established practice. He writes as follows:

Later on Tertullian writes that infant baptism was a cherished ecclesiastical practice and he even advocates it.[11]

This statement can nowhere be found in Tertullian's *On the Soul* (*De Anima*). Barnard gives the reference as *De Anima* 210,213. If Barnard had consulted the primary work, he would have noted that the reference '210,213' does not exist in *On*

---

[11] The original Afrikaans version reads as follows:
Later skryf hy (= Tertullianus) daarby dat die kinderdoop 'n geliefde kerklike gebruik is en pleit hy selfs daarvoor (*De Anima* 210,213). (Barnard 1984:80)

the *Soul* (*De Anima*) at all. As a matter of fact, most secondary books indicate the date of authorship of *On the Soul* as 210-213 (for example J. Quasten 1975:II.289). Barnard, however, probably seems to intend the figures '210,213' of the phrase '*De Anima* 210,213' at the end of the quotation as a reference to the passage and not to the date of authorship, since he uses this format in all the other quotations in his book.

Perhaps Barnard had the same passage in mind which is also referred to by Marais who says:

> No wonder that in a later work Tertullian dropped his objections against infant baptism in favour of the general practice of the Church.[12]

Marais then refers to Tertullian's *On the Soul* (*De Anima*) 39, though he does not quote it verbatim. The text in Tertullian runs as follows:

> On this principle of early possession it was that Socrates, while yet a boy, was found by the spirit of the demon. Thus, too, is it that to all persons their genii are assigned, which is only another name for demons. Hence in no case (I mean of the heathen, of course) is there any nativity which is pure of idolatrous superstition. It was from this circumstance that the apostle said, that when either of the parents was sanctified, the children were holy; and this as much by the prerogative of the seed as by the discipline of the institution. 'Else', says he, 'were the children unclean' by birth: as if he meant us to understand that the children of believers were designed for holiness, and thereby for salvation; in order that he might by the pledge of such a hope give his support to matrimony, which he

---

[12] The original Afrikaans version reads as follows:
G'n wonder nie dat Tertulianus (*sic*) dan ook in 'n later geskrif van hom sy besware teen die kinderdoop laat vaar het ten gunste van die algemene gebruik van die Kerk. (Marais 1974:72)

had determined to maintain in its integrity. Besides, he had certainly not forgotten what the Lord had so definitely stated: 'Except a man be born of water and of the Spirit, he cannot enter into the kingdom of God'; in other words, he cannot be holy. (Tertullian *On the Soul* 39)

It is unclear how Marais can use this passage as evidence that Tertullian eventually accepted infant baptism. The issue at stake in *On the Soul* 39 is not baptism, but demon possession (for a discussion of the above passage, see chapter 7).

Marais (1974:74) and Barnard (1984:79) also refer to Origen who stated that the rite of infant baptism was 'handed down by Christ and the apostles'. This phrase, however, was commonly used by ancient Patristic authors to appeal to the apostles or ancient leaders in order to give more authority to the point of view they were arguing. Thus Irenaeus (cf. chapter 5) appeals to the apostle John as authority for his statement that Jesus lived up to the time of Trajan (98-117 A.D.) Thus one should bear in mind that an ancient theologian is not necessarily correct when he claims that his beliefs are in line with the teaching of the apostles.

A noteworthy and well-known presentation of numerous passages on baptism, from the writings of early Church Fathers (as well as some inscriptions) was published in 1969 by Heinz Kraft (*Texte zur Geschichte der Taufe, besonders der Kindertaufe in der alten Kirche*). Some of these passages will be discussed in later chapters of this book. Kraft's book is an example of what is frequently found in such publications, namely, that passages are piled up giving the impression of numerous 'proofs', though in reality many of these quotations have nothing to do with the rite of baptism at all. However, they do contain phrases which, taken out of context, are believed by the authors to be on a par with phraseology they would understand to refer to infant baptism.

These passages (quoted by Kraft, and also by other scholars), have not been included in this book since they do not appear to contribute anything to the subject of the book. The following extract may illustrate the nature of such passages:

> For where the Church is, there is the Spirit of God; and where the Spirit of God is, there is the Church, and every kind of grace; but the Spirit is truth. Those, therefore, who do not partake of Him, are neither nourished into life from the mother's breasts, nor do they enjoy that most limpid fountain which issues from the body of Christ; but they dig for themselves broken cisterns out of earthly trenches, and drink putrid water out of the mire fleeing from the faith of the Church lest they be convicted; and rejecting the Spirit, that they may not be instructed. (Irenaeus *Against Heresies* 3,24,1)

No comment is required to show that this passage can in no way, by whatever stretch of one's imagination, be used as reference to substantiate any point of view on baptism in the early church.

By now it must be clear that many scholars are representing the history of the early church so as to suit their own theological presuppositions. The present authors have often been approached by Christians with questions regarding the practice of baptism in the early church. These Christians were usually perturbed and clearly confused because of the distorted statements which they have read in modern secondary works on this subject. It soon became evident that there is a very sincere need among modern Christians to read the primary texts (whether in the original language or in translation) on the practice of baptism in this very important era in our church history. This study is an attempt to make these sources accessible to all Christians in an objective way.

CHAPTER 2

The Apostolic Fathers

The term 'Apostolic Fathers' is used for a group of ecclesiastical authors who wrote their works before the middle of the second century. Ever since 1672, when J.B. Cotelier coined the term 'Apostolic Fathers', these works have always enjoyed a separate place in early Christian literature. Though there is no unanimity among scholars, the following authors generally pass for Apostolic Fathers: Papias of Hierapolis, Ignatius of Antioch, Clement of Rome, Polycarp of Smyrna, Barnabas, and the authors of *The Letter to Diognetus*, *The Shepherd of Hermas*, and *The Didache*. These writings are heterogeneous in character and do not really form a unity, but their early date is perhaps enough justification for the convention to treat them together. Only those writings of the Apostolic Fathers which contain statements relevant to this study will be treated here.

The Didache (or The Teaching of the Twelve Apostles)

The dating and composition of this document is shrouded in obscurity. Some scholars date it around the year 60 or 70, others at the turn of the first century, or in the first half of the second century. Still others place it in the latter part of the second century. Some even suppose that it is an archaistic work of a fourth century author who wanted to convey a picture of primitive church life and revive its relative informality in preaching and prayer. Others argue that it may be a genuine but late description of church life in a remote place, or of an eccentric group who managed to retain primitive elements in their worship. It is also possible that some parts of the work are of early date while other parts are later insertions. Consequently, the importance and relevance of this document for our study depend on the question of dating and whether its primitiveness is genuine or feigned. Since the majority of scholars still argue for a date in the first century, this work is included in this study.

The following passage is frequently cited in the modern debate on baptism, but it is seldom discussed in detail. Let us therefore scrutinize this section which runs as follows:

> And concerning baptism, baptize thus: Having first rehearsed all these things, baptize in the name of the Father, and of the Son, and of the Holy Spirit, in running water. But if you do not have running water, baptize into other water; and if you cannot in cold, then in warm. But if you have neither, pour water three times on the head in the name of Father and Son and Holy Spirit. But before the baptism let the baptizer fast, and the baptized, and any others who are able; but you must order the baptized to fast one or two days before. (*Didache* 7)

The words 'Having first rehearsed all these things' probably refer to a pre-baptismal catechetical instruction. But what is meant by 'all these things'? This probably refers to the preceding six chapters of *The Didache* which deal with 'The Two Ways' – the way of life and the way of death. Thus it seems that this pre-baptismal instruction consisted of moral and ethical norms for Christian life. Both the period of instruction, and the principles which had to be complied with, suggest that the baptismal candidates were people of responsibility.

One should note, however, that there is no mention of the redemptive work of Jesus, namely his passion, death and resurrection, neither in this passage on baptism, nor in the rest of the work. These are important elements of the creeds which were, since the earliest times, recited by candidates for baptism (cf. chapter 8). It is also doubtful that the 'rehearsing' should be understood as a kind of recitation of 'The Two Ways', as described in the first six chapters of *The Didache*. Perhaps the Greek word προλέγω should be translated as 'to state publicly', 'to proclaim' (cf. Liddell and Scott 1961:1488). It was indeed common practice for baptismal candidates to make public statements of their beliefs. It is also evident from this passage that fasting is part and parcel of the pre-baptismal instruction. This is in accordance with our explanation in chapter 1 that fasting was more than the mere abstinence from food. It was a period of prayer and spiritual dedication. This aspect of the pre-baptismal period automatically eliminates infants. Note that *The Didache* is not our only source of evidence on the relation between baptism and fasting (cf., for example, chapter 4).

It is also noteworthy that the author of *The Didache* does not address specific officiants when he gives his guidelines for the practice of baptism. As a matter of fact, a few lines earlier he has addressed all the believers and called them 'children' (chapter 5.2), a term which was used in ancient times for 'students' or 'disciples'.

The term 'running water' (literally 'living water') is usually understood as the water flowing in a river. This seems to be a very obvious interpretation. Concerning the phrase '... and if you cannot (baptize) in cold (water), then in warm', Marais argues as follows: 'The warm water refers to the water in the baptismal font.'[1] Oepke (as quoted in A. Vööbus 1968:23) goes even further and says that this is the water that has been warmed up for the baptism of children. But *The Didache* is nowhere speaking about children. Vööbus, however, offers a less forced and therefore a more plausible explanation. He says that the term 'cold water' is used to refer to the use of water from a river or spring, in other words water at its natural temperature. On the other hand, the term 'warm water' is used as 'a general characterization for water of a different kind, the kind

---

[1] The original Afrikaans version reads:
Die warm water dui op die water in 'n doopvont. (Marais 1974:143)

to be found in cisterns, pools and reservoirs. This is still water which has lost its natural temperature' (Vööbus 1968:24).

Concerning the mode of baptism *The Didache* is not very dogmatic. It is clear, however, that preference is given to immersion, but when sufficient water is not available, the affusion of water is allowed. It is also possible that the concessions to use warm water and to allow for affusion as a mode of baptism refer to clinical or emergency baptism. The term 'clinical baptism' (or emergency baptism) was used to refer to baptism which was administered to sick people in cases of necessity.

The author of *The Didache* does not only give us prescriptions on the practice of baptism, but he also tells us something about the significance of this sacrament. He writes as follows:

> But let no one eat or drink of your Eucharist, except those who have been baptized in the name of the Lord; for concerning this also the Lord has said, Give not that which is holy to the dogs. (*Didache* 9,5)

The author clearly regards baptism as a prerequisite for full membership in the congregation of believers which entitles the believer to participate in the eucharist. Note that in this passage it is stated that the person is baptized 'in the name of the Lord', while in the previous quotation the trinitarian formula was employed in the rite of baptism. Matthew 28:19 and *The Didache* are the earliest evidence for the use of the trinitarian formula in the act of baptism. It is evident from other literature that originally the shorter formula was used and that the trinitarian formula emerged in the middle of the second century. Scholars doubt whether the author of *The Didache* could have borrowed the trinitarian formula from Matthew since there is no other affinity between *The Didache* and the Gospel of Matthew. Consequently scholars argue that the text of *The Didache* was modified at a much later stage and the shorter formula was then replaced with the trinitarian formula.

The Epistle of Barnabas

According to tradition, the author of this work is Barnabas, the companion of Paul (Acts 4:36). Though the tradition is certainly mistaken, it is convenient to retain this title. The date of the *Epistle of Barnabas* is doubtful but it must have been written at the end of the first or the beginning of the second century.

The main objective of the work is to show that the Jews misunderstood the Scriptures because they interpreted the Mosaic laws literally. Barnabas proposes an allegorical interpretation of the Old Testament and argues that the sole purpose of these laws was to point forward to the Christian dispensation.

The author of the epistle believes that all the important elements of the new dispensation were foreshadowed in the Old Testament. He, for instance, sees the cross of Jesus in the outstretched arms of Moses (Ex. 17:11-12) and in the lifting up of the brazen serpent (Num. 21:9). At one stage he asks whether the water of baptism also was typified in the Old Testament. In his discussion of this matter, we do find some information on the practice of baptism during his time. He writes as follows:

1. Let us further inquire whether the Lord took any care to foreshadow the water (of baptism) and the cross. Concerning the water, indeed, it is written, in reference to the Israelites, that they should not receive that baptism which leads to the remission of sins, but should procure another for themselves. 2. The prophet therefore declares, 'Be astonished, O heaven, and let the earth tremble at this, because this people has committed two great evils: they have forsaken Me, the spring of life, and have hewn out for themselves broken cisterns. 3. Is my holy hill Zion a desolate rock? For you shall be as the fledglings of a bird, which fly away when the nest is removed.' 4. And again says the prophet, 'I will go before you and make level the mountains, and will break the

brazen gates, and bruise in pieces the iron bars; and I will give you the secret, hidden, invisible treasures, that they may know that I am the Lord God.' 5. And 'He shall dwell in a lofty cave of the strong rock.' Furthermore, what says He in reference to the Son? 'His water is sure; you shall see the King in His glory, and your soul shall meditate on the fear of the Lord.' 6. And again He says in another prophet, 'The man who does these things shall be like the tree, which is planted at the partings of the water, which shall yield its fruit in due season; and his leaf shall not fade, and all that he does shall prosper. 7. Not so are the ungodly, not so, but even as chaff, which the wind sweeps away from the face of the earth. Therefore the ungodly shall not stand in judgment, nor sinners in the counsel of the just; for the Lord knows the way of the righteous, but the way of the ungodly shall perish.' 8. Mark how He has described at once both the water and the cross. For he means this, Blessed are those who hoped on the cross, and descended into the water; for, says He, they shall receive their reward in due time: then He declares, I will recompense them. But now He says, 'Their leaves shall not fade.' This means, that every word which proceeds out of your mouth in faith and love shall tend to bring conversion and hope to many. 9. Again, another prophet says, 'And the land of Jacob shall be extolled above every land.' This means the vessel of His Spirit, which He shall glorify. 10. Further, what says He? 'And there was a river flowing on the right, and from it arose beautiful trees; and whosoever shall eat of them shall live for ever.' 11. This means, that we go down into the water full of sins and foulness, and we come up, bearing the fruit of fear in our hearts, and having hope on Jesus in the Spirit. 'And whosoever shall eat of these shall live for ever.' This means: Whosoever, He declares, shall hear you speaking, and believe, shall live for ever. (*Barnabas* 11)

In the first verse the author says that the Jews do not have the baptism that brings the remission of sins. The implication is that the Christians, on the other hand, do have this baptism. Thus we see in this statement too that baptism is linked to the remission of sins, and not to the covenant or circumcision. In the rest of the pericope the writer quotes a number of instances from the Old Testament to 'prove' that the water of baptism was foreshadowed in the Old Testament. All these 'proofs' are merely vague references to water, such as 'the *spring* of life' (verse 2), 'His *water* is sure' (verse 5), '... the tree, which is planted at the partings of the *waters*' (verse 6) and 'And there was a *river* flowing on the right' (verse 10). The author denies any literal interpretation to these verses and interprets them as references to baptism.

But in this passage there is more information concerning baptism as practised by the early Christians. In his interpretation of Psalm 1:3-6, the writer concludes that the meaning of this Psalm is essentially 'blessed are those who hoped on the cross, *and descended into the water.*' A few lines further on we again read 'This means, *that we go down into the water* full of sins and foulness, and *we come up*, bearing the fruit of fear in our hearts, and having hope on Jesus in the Spirit'.

The phrases 'going down into the water' and 'coming up' were used as technical terms for immersion. Some may argue that these phrases were merely used for descending and ascending the banks of a river or stream and that it does not necessarily imply that the baptismal candidates were immersed. These phrases frequently occur, however, in the early Christian literature and some of these occurrences undoubtedly refer to immersion. Note also that we read that the baptismal candidates are 'going down into the water'. It does seem from the statement concerning baptismal candidates who go down into the water, that they are doing so of their own accord.

The author says that the candidate is foul when he enters the water and thereafter he has 'the fruit of fear in his heart'. This is once again a reference to the cleansing character of baptism as a symbol of remission of sins.

The Shepherd of Hermas

We know almost nothing about Hermas, who, according to tradition, wrote this book. It is unlikely that this Hermas is the same person as the one mentioned by Paul in his letter to the Romans. Hermas wrote his work between A.D. 140 and 155. It was highly acclaimed in the early church and was widely regarded as scripture. This book consists of a series of visions or revelations which were made to Hermas by two heavenly figures, the first an old woman and the second an angel in the form of a shepherd. The main question treated in this work is that of the forgiveness of post-baptismal sin. Since the earliest times it was believed that baptism washes away sins and that one should lead a sinless life after baptism. It appears that Christians believed there was no remission of sins after baptism. Hermas, however, did not agree with such rigorism and argued that if one did continue to sin, forgiveness for post-baptismal sins could be obtained through repentance.

Let us look at one of the passages where Hermas deals with this problem. In this passage Hermas is in conversation with the angel of repentance who appeared as a shepherd:

> 1. And I said to him, 'I should like to continue my questions.' 'Speak on,' said he. And I said, 'I heard, sir, from some teachers that there is no other repentance than that which takes place, when we went down into the water and received remission of our former sins.' 2. He said to me, 'That was sound doctrine which you heard; for that is really the case. For he who has received remission of his sins ought not to sin any more, but to live in purity. 3. Since, however, you inquire diligently into all things, I will point this also out to you, not as giving occasion for error to those who are to believe, or have lately believed, in the

Lord. For those who have already believed, and those who are to believe, have no repentance of sins, but have remission of their previous sins. 4. For to those who have been called before these days, the Lord has set repentance. For the Lord, knowing the heart, and foreknowing all things, knew the weakness of men and the manifold wiles of the devil, that he would inflict some evil on the servants of God, and would act wickedly towards them. 5. The Lord, therefore, being merciful, has had mercy on the work of His hand, and has set repentance for them; and He has entrusted to me power over this repentance. 6. And therefore I say to you, that if any one is tempted by the devil, and sins after that great and holy calling in which the Lord has called His people to everlasting life, he has opportunity to repent but once. But if he should sin frequently after this, and then repent, to such a man his repentance will be of no avail; for with difficulty will he live.' (*The Shepherd* Mand. 4:3:1-6)

Hermas says that he has heard 'from some teachers that there is no other repentance'. Some scholars argue that he probably refers to Hebrews 6:4ff. (cf. Loeb Apostolic Fathers Vol. 2, p. 83). He might as well refer to the teachers in the group of believers to which he belongs. In verse 1 we again encounter the phrase 'going down into the water' expressing the idea of immersion. In the same verse there is again clear indication that baptism was linked to the remission of sins.

Though the form of this work is visionary and apocalyptic, its principal aim is to give practical and ethical guidelines to those who have been baptized so that they can live in purity. This already suggests that the baptismal candidates are people who can accept responsibility. As a matter of fact, these candidates have committed sins which need to be washed away and this surely makes it unlikely that infants are involved.

Note also that in verse 3 Hermas says that 'those who have already believed and those who are to believe, have no repentance of sins, but have remission of their previous sins.' The phrase 'remission of sins' was often used to refer to baptism as such. Thus the meaning of this statement is that those who *believe* get their opportunity to obtain remission of sins when they are *baptized.* It is evident that Hermas restricts baptism to believers.

In the ninth similitude Hermas compares the church with the construction of a tower. Many 'stones', i.e. people, are used to build this tower. He also alludes to the baptism of these 'stones' (i.e. people) in the following passage:

1. 'Explain to me a little further, sir,' I said. 'What is it that you desire?' he asked. 'Why, sir,' I said, 'did these stones ascend out of the pit, and be applied to the building of the tower, after having borne these spirits?' 2. 'They were obliged,' he answered, 'to ascend through water in order that they might be made alive; for, unless they laid aside the deadness of their life, they could not in any other way enter into the kingdom of God. 3. Accordingly, those also who fell asleep received the seal of the Son of God.' For, he continued, 'before a man bears the name of the Son of God he is dead; but when he receives the seal he lays aside his deadness, and obtains life. 4. The seal, then, is the water: they go down into the water dead, and they come up alive. And to them accordingly, was this seal preached, and they made use of it that they might enter into the kingdom of God.' 5. 'Why, sir,' I asked, 'did the forty stones also ascend with them out of the pit, having already received the seal?' 'Because,' he said, 'these apostles and teachers who preached the name of the Son of God, after falling asleep in the power and faith of the Son of God, preached it not only to those who were asleep, but themselves also gave them the seal of the preaching. 6. Accordingly they descended with them into the water, and again ascended. But these went down alive and came up again alive; whereas they who had

previously fallen asleep went down dead, but came up
again alive. 7. By these, then, were they quickened and
made to know the name of the Son of God. For this reason also did they ascend with them, and were fitted along
with them into the building of the tower, and, untouched
by the chisel, were built in along with them. For they slept
in righteousness and in great purity, but only they had
not this seal. You have accordingly the explanation of
these also.' (*The Shepherd* \ pard lang2057 Sim 9:16)

In this passage we once again read about the 'going down
into the water' and the 'coming up' thereafter. It is clear that
'coming up' definitely does not refer to 'ascending the banks' of
a river or stream after the administration of baptism. This is
evident from the Greek which reads εἰς τὸ ὕδωρ οὖν καταβαίνουσι and δι' ὕδατος ἀναβῆναι. Obviously the phrases 'going
down' and 'coming up' are used to focus on the two processes
involved in immersion.

This passage also tells us something about Hermas' theology
concerning baptism. In the first place he calls baptism 'a seal'
(verses 3-7). In verse 5 he even calls baptism 'the seal of the
preaching'. But what is the meaning of this phrase? It probably
means that the preaching of the Good News results in the
baptism (= seal) of those who accept it. Thus it would imply
that the baptismal candidates are people who are capable of
responding to the Gospel. Furthermore, Hermas regards
baptism as the death of one's former life and also the entering
of a new life. Moreover, Hermas is clearly convinced that
baptism is necessary for salvation. This explains why the
apostles and teachers descended to the abode of the dead to
baptize those who had died before the redeeming death of
Jesus. On another occasion too Hermas discloses that baptism
was necessary for salvation. In that instance he writes as follows:

Hear then why the tower is built upon the waters. It is
because your life has been, and will be, saved through

water (i.e. baptism). For the tower was founded on the word of the almighty and glorious Name, and it is kept together by the invisible power of the Lord.' (*The Shepherd* Vis. 3:3:5)

CHAPTER 3

Aristides of Athens

Aristides is one of the earliest apologists of Christianity. Very little is known about him, but in his *Apology* he describes himself as an 'Athenian philosopher'. Eusebius (*E.H.* 4,3,3) asserts that Aristides addressed his *Apology* to the Emperor Hadrian (117-138). Some modern-day scholars (cf. *The Oxford Dictionary of the Christian Church* 1978:84; Cross 1960:47), however, argue that it was addressed to Antoninus Pius (138-161) and that it probably dates from about the year 140. Aristides says nothing specifically on baptism, but is included here since he is often quoted in discussions on baptism in the early church.

It is interesting to note what statements scholars resort to in order to substantiate theological beliefs. Jeremias, for example, gives the following quotation from Aristides:

And when a child has been born to one of them they thank God; and if he dies in infancy, they thank him exceedingly, because he (= infant) departed this life without sins. (Aristides *Apology* 15.11)

Jeremias (1960:70ff.), who wants to prove infant baptism, argues that the phrase 'they thank God' alludes to infant baptism. He interprets this phrase on the basis of a similar phrase used in the same work of Aristides. It runs as follows:

And when it happens that one of them (the pagans) is converted, he is ashamed before the Christians of the works that he has done, and thanks God, saying, 'In ignorance have I done them'. And he purifies his heart, and his sins are forgiven him. (Aristides *Apology* 17.4)

Jeremias is convinced that in this second passage the phrase 'to thank God' undoubtedly refers to baptism. He thus concludes that it is 'very probable' that the quoted phrase should be interpreted likewise in the former instance. Jeremias' arguments in both places are unconvincing, if not far-fetched.

He nevertheless believes that his interpretation of the phrase 'they thank God' as an allusion to baptism, is confirmed by the phrase 'because the infant departed this life without sins'. Jeremias says that the latter phrase can hardly refer to the innocence of *childhood per se*, but should rather be interpreted as innocence because of the *remission of sins obtained through baptism*. But Jeremias is mistaken. The whole passage deals with the exemplary character of Christian lives where purity is acclaimed. Thus a baby who dies in infanthood can more easily attain this purity than an old man (regardless of his baptism). Aland's (1963:55-56) explanation of the term 'to thank God' is straightforward and to the point. He argues that it alludes to the thankfulness of the new convert for his conversion and does not signify any baptismal rite.

Aland, on the other hand, in his attempt to disprove the practice of infant baptism in the early church, resorts to another equally obscure statement of Aristides and interprets it as baptism of children at a more advanced age. He cites the following passage from Aristides' *Apology*:

Now they instruct the servants and maids or the children, when any of them have such, that they become Christians, on account of the love which they had for them. And when they have become Christians they call them brethren without distinction. (Aristides *Apology* 15.6)

Aland then comments as follows on this passage:

> According to Aristides, then, a baptism of these children while still infants is excluded, even though they come from Christian families (newly converted Christians are not here in view!) The impression is given that they are baptized only after they have attained the needful insight, hence not before they have become several years old. (Aland 1963:57)

Aland, too, is reading too much into the text. No responsible reader would be willing to discuss baptism in the early church based on such vague statements. Interpretations of this kind are always very risky. As a matter of fact, the interpretations of Jeremias and Aland, two scholars with opposing views concerning infant baptism, show how the same patristic writing can be employed to substantiate contradicting viewpoints. It would be much better and more valid to admit that Aristides' *Apology* does not bear any testimony to the doctrine of early Christian baptism. His work is an apology for the Christian faith and in it he points out the exemplary character of Christian morality. In fact, Aristides says that he intentionally avoids discussing any other matter (and this includes Christian doctrine). The latter, he says, can be found in other writings of the Christians. He contends as follows at the beginning of the last chapter:

> So much, O King, I have spoken; for concerning the rest, as has been said, words are to be found in their other writings which are much too difficult to be cited or repeated by anyone. (Aristides *Apology* 17.1)

It seems to be more in line with Aristides' own objective to refrain from scrutinizing his *Apology* for Christian doctrines and from basing far-fetched arguments on obscure verses. There are enough explicit references to baptism in other Patristic writings.

CHAPTER 4

Justin

Justin was born of pagan parents about A.D. 100 in Flavia Neapolis (formerly Shechem in Palestine). He first searched for the truth in pagan philosophies such as Stoicism, Peripateticism, Pythagoreanism and Platonism. Eventually, after a casual meeting with an old man on the sea-shore, he embraced Christianity. Justin, an itinerant evangelist, is the most notable of the Greek apologists of the second century. He composed two apologies for the Christian faith between 148 and 161 and addressed them to Emperor Antoninus Pius. Hereafter he wrote his *Dialogue with the Jew Trypho*. Justin was condemned because of his Christian faith and was beheaded about the year 165.

As has been indicated in the first chapter of this book, Justin is often cited as an early witness to infant baptism because of his statement that 'many, both men and women, who have been Christ's disciples from childhood, remain pure at the age of sixty or seventy years.' This statement has been discussed on pp. 5ff. above. It was also indicated that many scholars who quote the above-mentioned section fail to point out that in the same work Justin explicitly describes the baptism of believers. Let us now examine this section in detail. It reads as follows:

> I will also relate the manner in which we dedicated ourselves to God when we had been made new through Christ; lest, if we omit this, we seem to be unfair in the explanation we are making. As many as are persuaded

and believe that what we teach and say is true, and undertake to be able to live accordingly, are instructed to pray and to entreat God with fasting, for the remission of their sins that are past, we praying and fasting with them. Then they are brought by us where there is water, and are regenerated in the same manner in which we were ourselves regenerated. For, in the name of God, the Father and Lord of the universe, and of our Saviour Jesus Christ, and of the Holy Spirit, they then receive the washing with water. For Christ also said, 'Except you be born again, you shall not enter into the kingdom of heaven.' Now, that it is impossible for those who have once been born to enter into their mothers' wombs, is manifest to all. And how those who have sinned and repent shall escape their sins, is declared by Isaiah the prophet, as I wrote above; he thus speaks: 'Wash you, make you clean; put away the evil of your doings from your souls; learn to do well; judge the fatherless, and plead for the widow: and come and let us reason together, says the Lord. And though your sins be as scarlet, I will make them white like wool; and though they be as crimson, I will make them white as snow. But if you refuse and rebel, the sword shall devour you: for the mouth of the Lord has spoken it.'

And for this (rite) we have learned from the apostles this reason. Since at our birth we were born without our own knowledge or choice, by our parents coming together, and were brought up in bad habits and wicked training; in order that we may not remain the children of necessity and of ignorance, but may become the children of choice and knowledge, and may obtain in the water the remission of sins formerly committed, there is pronounced over him who chooses to be born again, and has repented of his sins, the name of God the Father and Lord of the universe; he who leads to the laver the person that is to be washed calling him by this name alone. For no one can utter the name of the ineffable God; and if any one dare to say that there is a name, he raves with a hopeless madness. And this washing is called illumination, because they who learn these things are illuminated in their understandings. And in the name of Jesus Christ, who was crucified under Pontius Pilate, and in the name of the Holy Ghost, who through the prophets foretold all things about Jesus, he who is illuminated is washed ... But we, after we have thus washed him who has been convinced and has assented to our teaching, bring him to the place where those who are called brethren are assembled, in order that we may offer hearty prayers in common for ourselves and for the baptized (illuminated) person, and for all others in every place, that we may be counted worthy, now that we have learned the truth, by our works also to be found good citizens and keepers of the commandments, so that we may be saved with an everlasting salvation. Having ended the prayers, we salute one another with a kiss. (Justin *Apology* 61,65)

In this passage Justin clearly spells out what the church of his time required from a person before he was accepted for baptism: Firstly, the person had to believe in the truth of the Christian doctrine; secondly, he had to undertake to live accordingly; thirdly, the baptismal candidate had to undergo a period of devotion and fasting in which he had to request God to forgive all his past sins. Note the sequence of events: An *acceptance* of the biblical truth which leads to a *commitment* to live accordingly; this is followed by a period of *devotion* which eventuates in *baptism*. Since only mature persons could satisfy these preconditions, it undoubtedly excludes the possibility that infants were involved in these activities. This is confirmed by the rest of the quotation in which it is stated that after the baptismal ceremony, the candidates were taken back to the congregation. In the section which follows the above quotation, Justin tells us

Justin

that these baptismal candidates were then allowed to partake of their first eucharist:

> And this food is called among us εὐχαριστία (the Eucharist), of which no one is allowed to partake but the man who believes that the things which we teach are true, and who has been washed with the washing (= baptized) that is for the remission of sins, and unto regeneration, and who is so living as Christ has enjoined. (Justin *Apology* I,66)

Justin says in the former passage that the baptismal candidate is taken to a place 'where there is water'. Since Christians assembled in houses for their worship services, they did not always have a baptistry or a place with much water readily available. Thus baptism was not necessarily practised at the place where they gathered for worship, but the baptismal candidates were rather taken to a place 'where there was water'. This would presumably be unnecessary if sprinkling was the mode of baptism, as this could be practised anywhere. Justin adds that after the baptismal ceremony the new convert is brought 'to the place where those who are called brethren are assembled'.

Justin then proceeds to discuss the necessity for remission of sins as a prerequisite for entrance into the kingdom of God. This shows that to Justin also there was a close relationship between baptism and the remission of sins. Justin did not see baptism as the means to obtain forgiveness of sins, since he explicitly says that one should entreat God to obtain remission of sins before one is allowed to enter the baptismal rite. Note also the different terms which were used for baptism, namely 'washing' and 'illumination' and that baptism was administered in the name of the triune God.

In the light of Justin's detailed discussion on baptism in the second century, it is surprising that modern scholars still endeavour to quote him as 'proof' for the practice of infant baptism. They ignore the above explicit accounts but prefer to resort to vague statements which can be interpreted either way.

CHAPTER 5

Irenaeus

We know very little about the life of Irenaeus who is commonly regarded as an important theologian of the second century. We do know that he was born between 140 and 160 and was a native of Asia Minor, perhaps Smyrna. He studied at Rome and later went to Gaul. During the persecution of 177, as presbyter of the church at Lyons, he carried a letter to Bishop Eleutherus in Rome requesting toleration for the Montanists of Asia Minor. He returned to Lyons in about 178 to find Bishop Pothinus had been martyred. Irenaeus became his successor. Apparently he died towards the end of the second century.

His chief work was his *Against Heresies* (*Adversus Haereses*). In this treatise he *inter alia* refutes the teaching of the Gnostics. In his treatment of the heretics, one gets insight into the orthodox point of view of his time. In the first book of *Against Heresies* he writes as follows:

> And when we come to refute them, we shall show in its fitting place, that this class of men have been instigated by Satan to a denial of that baptism which is a regeneration to God, and thus to a renunciation of the whole (Christian) faith. For some of them prepare a nuptial couch, and perform a sort of mystic rite (pronouncing certain expressions) with those who are being initiated, and affirm that it is a spiritual marriage which is celebrated by them, after the likeness of the conjunctions above. Others, again, lead them to a place where water

is, and baptize them, with the utterance of these words, 'Into the name of the unknown Father of the universe – into truth, the mother of all things – into Him who descended on Jesus – into union, and redemption, and communion with the powers.' Others still repeat certain Hebrew words, in order the more thoroughly to bewilder those who are being initiated, as follows: 'Basema, Chamosse, Baoenaora, Mistadia, Ruada, Kousta, Babaphor, Kalachthei.' (Irenaeus *Against Heresies* 1,21, 1&3)

In the pericope above Irenaeus charges the Marcosians with denying 'baptism which is a regeneration to God'. This clearly shows that Irenaeus regarded baptism as being 'a regeneration to God'. Note that Irenaeus says that the Marcosians used baptism, the nuptial couch and the repetition of certain Hebrew words, as initiation rites. In many religions baptism had this initiatory function. It seems that originally, in orthodox Christianity also, baptism was used to initiate a new convert into the circle of believers. Justin, for instance, tells us how those who accept Christianity are baptized before they are brought into the fellowship of believers to partake of their first eucharist (cf. chapter 4). Furthermore, it is interesting to note that the Gnostics, too, 'lead their followers to a place where water is'. The same was said of their orthodox brothers (cf. Justin's statement in chapter 4). Nevertheless, Irenaeus refutes the Gnostics because they denied the orthodox meaning of baptism (i.e. a regeneration to God) and introduced other initiatory rites. Moreover, unconventional acts accompanied their baptismal rites, for instance the repetition of certain Hebrew words.

C. De Beus (1948:193), Jeremias (1960:72ff.), Quasten (1975:I.311), *The Oxford Dictionary of the Christian Church* (1978:701), and many other supporters of infant baptism regularly refer to the following statement of Irenaeus as evidence for infant baptism in the early church:

For He (Jesus) came to save all through means of Himself
— all, I say, who through Him are born again to God —
infants, and children, and boys, and youths, and old
men. (Irenaeus *Against Heresies* 2,22,4)

Jeremias, for example, maintains that the phrase 'born again to God' must refer to baptism since the early church often linked baptism and regeneration, that is 'being born again'. If we had only these lines from Irenaeus the claim for infant baptism could perhaps be made, but the total context in which Irenaeus made this statement is against such a conclusion. It is rather pretentious to insist on substituting the notion of baptism every time a writer uses the term 'regeneration' unless the context clearly relates to baptism as such. One should first of all inquire into the *nature of the argument*, and since the quotation from Irenaeus has attracted so much attention, the passage from Irenaeus deserves such an inquiry.

In *Against Heresies* (book 2) Irenaeus refutes the teachings of the Valentinians and the Marcionites, prominent Christian sects at the time. They claimed that supernatural powers (called Aeons) not only created the world but also regulated all events. They maintained that when Jesus was baptized at the age of thirty, this number of years corresponds to thirty Aeons called 'the silent Aeons' in their system.

According to these heretics the Aeons caused Jesus to become the Christ at his baptism. Then a group of twelve Aeons caused him to preach for only one year after his baptism. The argument of these heretics are refuted by Irenaeus in *Against Heresies* (book 2, chapter 22) by referring to traditions, handed down from the apostles, that Jesus preached at least to fifty years of age. Irenaeus even declares that Jesus lived until the time of the Emperor Trajan (*Against Heresies*, book 2, chapter 22,5) which would have made Jesus an old man of ninety years or more. This gross exaggeration was how Irenaeus counter-argued the one year claim of the heretics. He thereby intended to illustrate that Jesus lived through all the ages of man, since the point he wanted to defend was that during the earthly ministry of Jesus, he was the Christ from birth to death, not merely for a period of twelve months following his thirtieth year. Thus, to say that through him every age received his redemptive work is to emphasize the fact that Jesus was the Christ from beginning to end – and his old age especially made him a Master according to Jewish tradition.

The passage from Irenaeus, quoted in full, clearly illustrates the issues explained above:

> Being thirty years old when He came to be baptized, and then possessing the full age of a Master, He came to Jerusalem, so that He might be properly acknowledged by all as a Master. For He did not seem one thing while He was another, as those affirm who describe Him as being man only in appearance; but what He was, that He also appeared to be. Being a Master, therefore, He also possessed the age of a Master, not despising or evading any condition of humanity, nor setting aside in Himself that law which He had appointed for the human race, but sanctifying every age, by that period corresponding to it which belonged to Himself. *For He came to save all through means of Himself - all, I say, who through Him are born again to God - infants, and children, and boys, and youths, and old men* (italics mine). He therefore passed through every age, becoming an infant for infants, thus sanctifying infants; a child for children, thus sanctifying those who are of this age, being at the same time made to them an example of piety, righteousness, and submission; a youth for youths, becoming an example to youths, and thus sanctifying them for the Lord. So likewise He was an old man for old men, that He might be a perfect Master for all, not merely as respects the setting forth of the truth, but also as regards age, sanctifying at the same time the aged also, and becoming an example to them likewise. Then, at last, He came on to death itself,

that He might be ' the first-born from the dead, that in all things He might have the pre-eminence,' the prince of life, existing before all, and going before all.

The single sentence (printed in italics in the quotation above), which is often quoted, merely tells us that the redeeming work of Christ extends to whatever person. The string 'infants and children and boys and youths and old men' is an inclusive statement to emphasize that everyone is involved. Its purpose is to show that in terms of the issue he disputes, the Christ in Jesus passed through every age. (Note that Irenaeus says this explicitly in the above passage). The passage does not speak about the age when people were baptized. In fact the passage does not refer to baptism as such but to Christ's redeeming work in an exaggerated framework in order to meet the arguments of his opponents that Jesus was the Christ for a period of twelve months only.

CHAPTER 6

Clement of Alexandria

Titus Flavius Clemens was born of pagan parentage about the year 150. He probably received his education in Athens. Clement travelled to Italy, Syria and Palestine in search of Christian teachers. Finally in Alexandria he met the eminent Pantaenus, for whom he had great respect. He became a pupil of and collaborator with Pantaenus and eventually in 200 succeeded him as the head of the school of catechumens in Alexandria.

When the persecution under Severus broke out about 203, Clement withdrew from Alexandria. He took refuge in Cappadocia where he died around 215 without ever having returned to Egypt.

In his attempt to prove infant baptism in the early church, Kraft quotes some passages from Clement to support his contention that infant baptism was practised from a very early stage. Among these we find the following passage which is quoted here more fully:

> But men are not to wear the ring on the joint; for this is feminine; but to place it on the little finger at its root. For so the hand will be freest for work, in whatever we need it; and the signet will not very easily fall off, being guarded by the large knot of the joint. And let our seals be either a dove, or a fish, or a ship scudding before the wind, or a musical lyre, which Polycrates used, or a ship's anchor, which Seleucus got engraved as a device; and if

there be one fishing, he will remember the apostle, and the children drawn out of the water. For we are not to delineate the faces of idols, we who are prohibited to cleave to them; nor a sword, nor a bow, following as we do, peace; nor drinking-cups, being temperate. (*The Educator* III,11 or 59)

The use of the word 'children' in this passage has tempted many scholars to understand it as referring to infants, yet even Jeremias has doubts on such an interpretation. In his attempt to defend infant baptism Jeremias (1960:64-5) appealed also to Church Fathers in Egypt and said: 'Here (in Egypt) we are on firmer ground'. Yet Clement is to him an exception and therefore he says: 'We shall indeed do well to disregard Clement of Alexandria. For when soon after 195 he speaks, in an allegorical figure, of the 'children who are drawn from the water' (by the fisherman) ... it is indeed possible that he is thinking of child baptism, but he might be thinking of children in the faith (cf. 1 Peter 2.1ff.) whom the missionary brings to baptism'.

It is quite possible that the words 'fisherman' and 'children drawn out of the water' function as baptismal terminology. On the other hand, it is also possible that Clement is building on the figurative expression of Jesus 'I will make you fishers of men' (Mt. 4:19) by referring to converts as 'children drawn out of water'. It is interesting that Jeremias comments on 'children' but that he is silent upon the phrase 'drawn out of water' which could be interpreted as immersion. Nevertheless, the term 'children' is most probably a figurative expression for new believers and therefore called 'children in the faith'. As a matter of fact, even Jeremias himself concedes that this is a possible interpretation referring to I Peter 2.1ff. for a similar usage of the phrase. Moreover, there are more examples of this figurative phrase in Clement's own writings, such as the following:

Truly, then, are we the children of God, having put off the old man and the cloak of wickedness, and having put on the immortality of Christ; that we may become a new, holy people by regeneration, and may keep the man undefiled. And a babe, as God's little one, is cleansed from fornication and wickedness. (*The Educator* I,6 or 32)

In this passage Clement is clearly using the phrases 'little ones' and 'children' figuratively. Perhaps this passage, too, refers to baptism. Simon Wood (*Fathers of Church* 1954:32n), for example, says that the phrase 'having put off the old man and the cloak of wickedness' is most probably a reference to a rite in the baptismal ceremony at which the clothes were put off as a symbol of one's former life. Nevertheless, whether this passage refers to baptism or to conversion, the term 'children of God' is undoubtedly used figuratively.

But there are more passages in Clement's writings which deal with baptism but which were unfortunately 'disregarded' by Jeremias. In the next section Clement, countering the attacks of the Gnostics, again uses the figurative expression 'children' and 'little ones' when he refers to baptismal practices:

We have ample means of encountering those who are given to carping. For we are not termed children and little ones with reference to the childish and contemptible character of our education, as those who are inflated on account of knowledge have calumniously alleged. Straightaway, on our regeneration, we attained that perfection after which we aspired. For we were illuminated, which is to know God. He is not then imperfect who knows what is perfect. And do not reprehend me when I profess to know God; for so it was deemed right to speak to the Word, and He is free. For at the moment of the Lord's baptism there sounded a voice from heaven, as a testimony to the Beloved, 'You are My beloved Son, today have I become your Father.' Let us then ask the wise,

Is Christ, begotten today, already perfect, or - what were most monstrous - imperfect? If the latter, there is some addition He requires yet to make. But for Him to make any addition to His knowledge is absurd, since He is God. For none can be superior to the Word, or the teacher of the only Teacher. Will they not then own, though reluctant, that the perfect Word born of the perfect Father was begotten in perfection, according to economic fore-ordination? And if He was perfect, why was He, the perfect one, baptized? It was necessary, they say, to fulfil the profession that pertained to humanity. Most excellent. Well, I assert, simultaneously with His baptism by John, He becomes perfect? Manifestly. He did not then learn anything more from him? Certainly not. But He is perfected by the washing - of baptism - alone, and is sanctified by the descent of the Spirit? Such is the case. The same also takes place in our case, whose exemplar Christ became. Being baptized, we are illuminated; illuminated, we become sons; being made sons, we are made perfect; being made perfect, we are made immortal. 'I' says He, 'have said that you are gods, and all sons of the Highest.' This work is variously called grace, and illumination, and perfection, and washing: washing, by which we cleanse away our sins; grace, by which the penalties accruing to transgressions are remitted; and illumination, by which that holy light of salvation is beheld, that is, by which we see God clearly. Now we call that perfect which wants nothing. For what is yet wanting to him who knows God? For it were truly monstrous that that which is not complete should be called a gift (or act) of God's grace. Being perfect, He consequently bestows perfect gifts. As at His command all things were made, so on His bare wishing to bestow grace, ensues the perfecting of His grace. For the future of time is anticipated by the power of His volition. (*The Educator* I,6 or 25-6)

In the first place, Clement says that one who is being baptized is being made perfect. As he himself explains, baptism is called 'perfection' because through baptism Jesus' command to man to be baptized is being fulfilled. Thus even Jesus was made 'perfect' through baptism, not because he was defective or lacking anything before baptism, but because he complied with his own command. Note also that Clement says that Jesus was 'washed' when he was baptized.

As in the case of the other Church Fathers, Clement too refers to baptism as 'illumination' and 'cleansing' and he believes that baptism washes away sins. Since conversion was always followed by baptism, the Church Fathers regarded these two acts as being closely related. Consequently terms such as 'illumination' ('enlightenment') or 'rebirth' ('regeneration') were used for either conversion or baptism. The latter two issues were regarded as almost simultaneous acts. This can also be seen in the next section:

> And he who is only regenerated - as the name necessarily indicates - and is enlightened, is delivered forthwith from darkness, and on the instant receives the light. As, then, those who have shaken off sleep forthwith become all awake within; or rather, as those who try to remove a film that is over the eyes, do not supply to them from without the light which they do not possess, but removing the obstacle from the eyes, leave the pupil free; thus also we who are baptized, having wiped off the sins which obscure the light of the Divine Spirit, have the eye of the spirit free, unimpeded, and full of light, by which alone we contemplate the Divine, the Holy Spirit flowing down to us from above. (*The Educator* I,6 or 27-8)

The same ideas on baptism are also expressed in the following section:

We are washed from all our sins, and are no longer entangled in evil. This is the one grace of illumination, that our characters are not the same as before our washing. And since knowledge springs up with illumination, shedding its beams around the mind, the moment we hear, we who were untaught become disciples. Does this, I ask, take place on the advent of this instruction? You cannot tell the time. For instruction leads to faith, and faith with baptism is trained by the Holy Spirit. (*The Educator* I,6 or 29-30)

The following section is generally interpreted as a reference to the rite in the baptismal ceremony in which milk and honey were given to the newly baptized:

With milk, then, the Lord's nutriment, we are nursed directly when we are born; and as soon as we are regenerated, we are honoured by receiving the good news of the hope of rest, even the Jerusalem above, in which it is written that milk and honey fall in showers, receiving through what is material the pledge of the sacred food. 'For meats are done away with,' as the apostle himself says; but this nourishment on milk leads to the heavens, rearing up citizens of heaven, and members of the angelic choirs. (*The Educator* I,6 or 45)

The following passage is probably another reference to the practice of giving milk and honey to those who were baptized. This interpretation is strengthened by the occurrence of baptismal terms such as 'reborn' and 'rebirth'.

Milk is the source of nourishment; by its presence a woman is shown to have brought forth a child, and to be truly a mother, by which also she receives a potent charm of affection. Wherefore the Holy Spirit in the apostle, using the voice of the Lord, says mystically, 'I have given you milk to drink.' For if we have been regenerated unto Christ, He who has regenerated us nourishes us with His own milk, the Word; (*The Educator* I,6 or 49)

But Jeremias also 'disregarded' another work of Clement which might have relevance for his study. Eusebius (H.E. vi.13) tells us that Clement wrote a work entitled *Exhortation to Endurance* or *To the Recently Baptized.* Baptism as a rite is not mentioned in this book by Clement, though the alternate title may suggest it. Clement merely issues clear precepts to those who had been baptized. In it he pictures the ideal of Christian conduct. It thus seems that Clement was thinking of baptismal candidates who were mature enough to bear this responsibility.

CHAPTER 7

Tertullian

Tertullian was born in Carthage of pagan priests about the middle of the second century. He received a good education and probably practised as a lawyer. Tertullian lived in licentiousness until about 193 when he was converted to Christianity. He then began to employ his expert knowledge in the service of the Christian faith.

Tertullian is the author of a wide range of apologetic, theological and ascetic works, all of which were written between 197 and 220. It is not known when he died but some scholars suggest a date between 240 and 250. It seems that a date closer to 220, when his literary activities ceased, is more likely, however.

In about 207 Tertullian joined the Montanists. He left his own imprint on these people to the extent that the North African Montanists were later known as 'Tertullianists'. Excerpts from Tertullian's writings are included in this study, despite his affinity with the Montanists, since he was an important theologian of the early church. He played a tremendous role in the development of the theology of the orthodox church. The Church Fathers had great respect for the excellence of Tertullian's writings and we know that Cyprian (third century) read his works daily. Moreover, the aberrations of the Montanists were more concerned with aspects of discipline and morality, than with doctrine or dogmatic issues. Tertullian's teaching on baptism was indeed in line with the teaching of the orthodox church.

In fact, in one of his works *The Chaplet (De Corona)*, written in about 211, Tertullian explicitly states that they practised baptism according to an unwritten tradition which was received by the common church. The main theme of this writing (*The Chaplet*) deals with the wearing of a military wreath by Christians. Tertullian argues that the wearing of crowns was incompatible with the Christian faith and as proof he resorts to an unwritten Christian tradition showing that it was unnatural to put a chaplet on the head. Since some might doubt the validity of an argument based on an unwritten tradition, Tertullian decides to demonstrate the power of tradition in other matters. He then refers to baptism as an example since the Scriptures do not elaborate on the particulars of the baptismal ceremony. Tertullian continues as follows:

> If no passage of Scripture has prescribed it, assuredly custom, which without doubt flowed from tradition, has confirmed it. For how can anything come into use, if it has not first been handed down? Even in pleading tradition, written authority, you say, must be demanded. Let us inquire, therefore, whether tradition, unless it be written, should not be admitted. Certainly we shall say that it ought not to be admitted, if no cases of other practices which, without any written instrument, we maintain on the ground of tradition alone, and the countenance thereafter of custom, affords us any precedent. To deal with this matter briefly, I shall begin with baptism. When we are going to enter the water, but a little before, in the presence of the congregation and under the hand of the president, we solemnly profess that we disown the devil, and his pomp, and his angels. Hereupon we are thrice immersed, making a somewhat ampler pledge than the Lord has appointed in the Gospel. Then, when we are taken up, we taste first of all a mixture of milk and honey, and from that day we refrain from the daily bath for a whole week. We take also, in congregations before day-

break, and from the hand of none but the presidents, the sacrament of the Eucharist, which the Lord both commanded to be eaten at meal-times, and he enjoined to be taken by all alike. (*The Chaplet* 3)

This description of the practice of baptism is remarkably similar to the descriptions found in the writings of other Church Fathers such as have already been discussed in the preceding chapters. Note again that the baptismal candidates were requested to denounce publicly the devil and his angels immediately before the baptismal ceremony. This procedure, found in many of the Fathers of the Church, made it unlikely that babies too were involved in the act of baptism.

The Oxford Dictionary of the Christian Church (1978:1388) says that 'the occasional references in early Christian literature to an 'unwritten tradition' left by the apostles appear to relate not to any body of information independent of Scripture, but to the evidence of Christian institutions and customs which confirms Scriptural teaching.' It is interesting to note that both Origen and Tertullian appeal to tradition to give authority to their doctrine on baptism. Origen, however, wants to prove infant baptism (cf. chapter 9), while Tertullian tells us that the tradition prescribes the baptism of people who have made a public confession of their faith. It was popular among early writers to appeal to the (apostolic) tradition to validate their cause. Therefore one cannot rely too much on the claims made unless the actual practice substantiates the claim. As such, when we look at the other extant accounts of baptism in the early church, Tertullian's report on baptism appears to be more in line with the practice of other churches in the first two centuries. Nevertheless, it is not the claim for tradition that is vital; it is the description of what actually happened during a baptismal service that really matters. Note also that several Church Fathers tell us that the neophytes celebrated the eucharist after their baptism.

In another writing of Tertullian he again tells us about the public confession which was made during the baptismal ceremony:

> Lest any one think that we are dealing in mere argumentative subtleties, I shall turn to that highest authority of our 'seal' itself. When entering the water, we make profession of the Christian faith in the words of its rule; we bear public testimony that we have renounced the devil, his pomp, and his angels. (*The Shows* 4)

In the above-quoted passage, baptism is again referred to as a 'seal'. In the following section Tertullian admonishes Christians not to partake of that which they have renounced in their baptismal vows. Tertullian frequently comes back to the responsibility which should be displayed by Christians after their baptism.

> We should have no connection with the things which we abjure, whether in deed or word, whether by looking on them or looking forward to them; but do we not abjure and rescind that baptismal pledge, when we cease to bear its testimony? (*The Shows* 24)

Tertullian was the first Church Father who wrote a full treatise on baptism. In fact, this work is the only ante-Nicene writing on any of the sacraments. It is therefore of great importance for this study. Unfortunately, because of practical reasons, it is not possible to quote the entire work in this study. We will, however, look at some excerpts which will give the reader a good insight into the essence of this important work, which was probably written between 198 and 200.

One of the most frequently quoted passages from this work (*On Baptism*) has been discussed in chapter 1 of this study. Let us now look at other lesser known sections from this work. In the first place, Tertullian, as all the other Church Fathers, believed that baptism 'washes away sins':

> Happy is our sacrament of water, in that, by washing away the sins of our early blindness, we are set free and admitted into eternal life! A treatise on this matter will not be superfluous; instructing not only such as are just becoming formed (in the faith), but them who, content with having simply believed, without full examination of the grounds of the traditions, carry (in mind), through ignorance, an untried though probable faith. (*On Baptism* 1)

In this same work Tertullian says that the baptismal ceremony was a simple act of some type of immersion:

> ... so that from the very fact, that with so great simplicity, without pomp, without any considerable novelty of preparation, finally, without expense, a man is dipped in water, and amid the utterance of some few words, is wetted, and then rises again, not much (or not at all) cleaner, the consequent attainment of eternity is esteemed the more incredible. (*On Baptism* 2)

In some translations the section above is rendered as '... a man is dipped in water, and amid the utterance of some few words, is *sprinkled*, and then rises again...' However, the Latin word *tinctus* (from *tingo*) never means 'to scatter a liquid in small drops' (that is, 'to sprinkle' but rather 'to imbue with a liquid', that is, 'to make thoroughly wet'. From the whole context it is clear that the candidate was probably immersed or at least properly wetted. This is also suggested by the following remark:

> And accordingly it makes no difference whether a man be washed in a sea or a pool, a stream or a fount, a lake or a

> trough ... Albeit the similitude may be admitted to be suitable to the simple act; that, since we are defiled by sins, as it were by dirt, we should be washed from those stains in waters. (*On Baptism* 4)

It seems from the above quotation that the only prerequisite was that the act of baptism should properly illustrate the 'washing' of the believer.

Tertullian, too, tells us about an unction after the act of baptism:

> After this, when we have issued from the font, we are thoroughly anointed with a blessed unction ... Thus, too, in our case, the unction runs carnally, (i.e. on the body), but profits spiritually; in the same way as the act of baptism itself too is carnal, in that we are plunged in water, but the effect spiritual, in that we are freed from sins. (*On Baptism* 7)

The above excerpt, in referring to 'being plunged in water' (Latin *in aqua mergimur*) again furnishes proof of some type of immersion as the regular mode of baptism and of the concept that baptism 'washed away' sins.

After the unction, hands were laid on the baptismal candidates:

> In the next place the hand is laid on us, invoking and inviting the Holy Spirit through benediction. (*On Baptism* 8)

Tertullian also argues that one occasion of baptism is sufficient; it needs not be repeated. Note especially the reason, namely, that after baptism a person should not sin again.

> We enter, then, the font once: once are sins washed away, because they ought never to be repeated. But the Jewish Israel bathes daily, because he is daily being defiled. (*On Baptism* 15)

One, however, should be careful not to appeal to this statement in the modern-day debate on rebaptism since the symbolical meaning of baptism in the early church differs significantly from the covenant baptism that developed later on.

Tertullian gives us very interesting information regarding the administrators of baptism. He says that anyone (i.e. the bishop, presbyters, deacons and even laymen), was allowed to baptize. Only women were excluded. Tertullian says:

> For concluding our brief subject, it remains to put you in mind also of the due observance of giving and receiving baptism. Of giving it, the chief priest (who is the bishop) has the right: in the next place, the presbyters and deacons, yet not without the bishop's authority, on account of the honour of the Church, which being preserved, peace is preserved. Beside these, even laymen have the right; for what is equally received can be equally given. Unless bishops, or priests, or deacons, be on the spot, other disciples are called i.e. to the work. The word of the Lord ought not to be hidden by any: in like manner, too, baptism, which is equally God's property, can be administered by all ... But if the writings which wrongly go under Paul's name, claim Thecla's example as a licence for women's teaching and baptizing, let them know that, in Asia, the presbyter who composed that writing, as if he were augmenting Paul's fame from his own store, after being convicted, and confessing that he had done it from love of Paul, was removed from his office. For how credible would it seem, that he who has not permitted a woman even to learn with overboldness, should give a female the power of teaching and baptizing! 'Let them be

silent,' he says, 'and at home consult their own husbands.' (*On Baptism* 17)

We know from other Church Fathers also that the early Christians favoured Passover for the administration of baptism (cf. chapters 8 and 22). Tertullian shared this view but he nevertheless admits that there was no distinction between a baptism that was administered during Passover and a baptism that was administered on any other day:

> The Passover affords a more than usually solemn day for baptism: when, withal, the Lord's Passion, in which we are baptized, was completed. Nor will it be incongruous to interpret figuratively the fact that, when the Lord was about to celebrate the last Passover, He said to the disciples who were sent to make preparation, 'You will meet a man bearing water.' He points out the place for celebrating the Passover by the sign of water. After that, Pentecost is a most joyous space for conferring baptisms ... However, every day is the Lord's; every hour, every time, is apt for baptism: if there is a difference in the solemnity, distinction there is none in the grace. (*On Baptism* 19)

Tertullian concludes this treatise on the baptism by repeating stringent injunctions to be obeyed by the baptismal candidates:

> They who are about to enter baptism ought to pray with repeated prayers, fasts, and bendings of the knee, and vigils all the night through, and with the confession of all bygone sins, that they may express the meaning even of the baptism of John: 'They were baptized,' says (the Scripture), 'confessing their own sins' ... 'Then,' someone will say, 'it becomes us, too, rather to fast after baptism.' Well, and who forbids you, unless it be the necessity for joy, and the thanksgiving for salvation? (*On Baptism* 20)

The belief that baptism washes away all sins undoubtedly gave rise to the practice of delaying baptism. The same Tertullian who admonished Christians not to baptize infants (see chapter 1), also criticized the delaying of baptism. He argues that baptism should follow immediately after repentance, i.e. after the heart of a person has been washed:

> Moreover, a presumptuous confidence in baptism introduces all kinds of vicious delay and neglect with regard to repentance: for, feeling sure of undoubted pardon of their sins, men meanwhile steal the intervening time, and make it for themselves into a holidaytime for sinning, rather than a time for learning not to sin. Further, how inconsistent is it to expect pardon of sins (to be granted) to a repentance which they have not fulfilled! ... That baptismal washing is a sealing of faith, which faith is begun and is commended by the faith of repentance. We are not washed in order that we may cease sinning, but because we have ceased, since in heart we have been bathed already. (*On Repentance* 6)

Despite all the above statements which clearly illustrate that Tertullian believed that only those who were mature enough to keep their baptismal vows should be baptized, some scholars try to find statements which could perhaps support modern views. They would, for example, quote the following sentence:

> It was from this circumstance that the apostle said, that when either of the parents was sanctified, the children were holy; and this as much by the prerogative of the seed as by the discipline of the institution. (*On the Soul* 39)

Jeremias (1960:84-5) says the following with regard to this section: 'Clearly Tertullian here does not only presuppose the practice of infant baptism, but he advocates it.' Barnard

(1984:80) probably also has this section in mind when he refers to Tertullian's *On the Soul* and comments as follows: 'Later on Tertullian writes that infant baptism was a cherished ecclesiastical practice and he even advocates it.'[1] (For this assumed statement, which in fact does not occur in Tertullian, see also chapter 1). But these scholars should look at the context in which this statement occurs. Aland (1963:64-7) has rightly argued that in the context preceding this quotation, Tertullian merely says that pagan superstition almost automatically makes the baby, who is born from heathen parents, the prey of the devil. But, according to the section above, for him who has Christian parents, even if only one of them is a Christian, this danger does not exist since he is born 'holy'. But Tertullian adds that this protection is obtained not only through one's 'seed' (i.e. one's descent from a Christian parent) but also through 'the discipline of the institution' (i.e. one's future education in Christian doctrine). The argument has nothing to do with baptism at all.

Thus it is unclear how this statement of Tertullian can be used to 'prove' that Tertullian advocated infant baptism, while the numerous explicit discussions on baptism in the writings of Tertullian, referred to above, are ignored.

---

[1] The original Afrikaans version reads as follows:

Later skryf hy (= Tertullianus) daarby dat die kinderdoop 'n geliefde kerklike gebruik is en pleit hy selfs daarvoor.

CHAPTER 8

Hippolytus

Hippolytus, born about 170, was an eminent theologian of the Roman Church in the third century. When Callistus was elected bishop in 217, Hippolytus came into conflict with him. Hippolytus then withdrew from the Roman Church and was made bishop of Rome by a small group of influential followers, thus becoming the first anti-pope.

This schism continued even during the reign of Callistus's successors, viz. Urban and Pontianus. In 235 Emperor Maximinus Thrax exiled both Hippolytus and Pontianus who seem to have become reconciled to each other in exile before they both died soon after. The church was again united, and elected Anterus as bishop. His successor brought the remains of these two men back to Rome. Hippolytus was the only one of a number of anti-popes of various times to whom the Roman Church has accorded the title *Sanctus* (= 'Holy'). Nevertheless, many of his works have survived in translation only.

Hippolytus is now generally considered by modern scholars to be the author of the *Apostolic Tradition*, which was formerly known as the *Egyptian Church Order*. It was originally written in Greek, but only a few small fragments survived. However, our main source for this work is a Latin translation from the fourth century. There are also Sahidic, Arabic, Ethiopic and Boharic versions of this work. This document, which was composed about the year 217, consists mainly of regulations for church organization and the conduct of worship. It thus also gives regulations on the rite of baptism in the Church of Rome in the beginning of the third century. Hippolytus writes as follows:

> They who are accepted for baptism shall be chosen after their lives have been examined: whether they have lived in honesty while they were catechumens, whether they have honoured widows, whether they have visited the sick, whether they have been active in good deeds. When those who brought them have testified that they have done these things, then let them hear the Gospel. Then from the time that they are separated (from the other catechumens), hands shall be laid upon them daily in exorcism. When the day of their baptism draws near, the bishop shall exorcise each one of them so that he may be assured of their purity. Then, if there is any one of them who is not good or pure, he shall be put aside because he has not heard the word in faith; for it is not possible for the alien to remain concealed. Then those who are about to be baptized need to be instructed to bathe and free themselves from impurity and wash themselves on Thursday. If a woman is menstruous, she shall be set aside and receive baptism on some other day.
> They who are to receive baptism shall fast on Friday. On Saturday the bishop shall assemble them in one place. He will command all of them to kneel in prayer. And, laying his hand upon them, he shall exorcise all alien spirits to flee from them and never to return. And when he has exorcized them he shall breathe in their faces, seal their foreheads, ears and noses, and then raise them up. They shall spend the whole night in vigil, listening to reading and instruction.
> They who are to be baptized shall bring with them no other vessel than the one each will bring for the eucharist; for it is becoming that he who is considered worthy of baptism should bring his offering at that hour.

At cockcrow prayer shall then be made over the water. The water shall flow through the baptismal pool or pour into it from above. Let it happen in this way except when there is scarcity of water. When there is scarcity, whether constant or occasional, then use whatever water you can find.

When they have removed their clothing, then first baptize the little ones. Those who can speak for themselves, shall do so; if not, their parents or some other relative shall speak for them. Then baptize the men, and last of all the women after they have loosened their hair and have put aside their gold or silver ornaments that they were wearing. No one should take any alien thing down to the water with them.

At the hour set for baptism the bishop gives thanks over oil which he puts into a container. He calls this the 'oil of thanksgiving'. He shall also take other oil and exorcise it. He calls this the 'oil of exorcism'. A deacon then brings the oil of exorcism, and stands at the left hand of the presbyter. Another deacon takes the oil of thanksgiving, and stands at the presbyter's right hand. Then the presbyter, takes hold of each of those who are about to be baptized. He shall then order him to renounce, saying:

'I renounce you, Satan, and all your servants and all your works.'

And when each one has renounced, he (the presbyter) anoints him with the oil of exorcism, saying: 'Let every spirit depart from you.'

Doing this, let him give him over naked to the bishop or presbyter who baptizes, and let the candidate stand in the water. Likewise let a deacon descend with him. And when he who is being baptized descends into the water, let him who baptizes him lay his hand on him saying thus:

'Do you believe in God, the Almighty Father?'

And he who is being baptized shall say:

'I believe.'
Then immediately, holding his hand placed on his head, he shall baptize him once. And then he shall say:
'Do you believe in Christ Jesus, the Son of God, who was born of the Holy Spirit of the Virgin Mary, and was crucified under Pontius Pilate, and was dead and buried, and on the third day He arose alive from the dead and ascended into heaven, and sat at the right hand of the Father, and will come to judge the living and the dead?'
And when he says:
'I believe,'
he is baptized again. And again he shall say:
'Do you believe in the Holy Spirit, and the holy church, and the resurrection of the flesh?'
He who is being baptized shall say:
'I believe,'
and so he is baptized a third time.
And thereafter, when he has ascended from the water, he is anointed by the presbyter with that oil that has been sanctified. The presbyter then says:
'I anoint you with holy oil in the name of Jesus Christ,'
And so each one, after drying himself, is clothed, and thereafter they enter the church.

Then the bishop, laying his hand upon them, shall pray, saying:
'O Lord God, who has made them worthy to obtain remission of sins through the bath of regeneration of the Holy Spirit, send into them your grace, that they may serve you according to your will. For yours is the glory: to the Father and the Son, with the Holy Spirit in the holy church, both now and for ever more. Amen.'
Thereafter, pouring the oil of thanksgiving from his hand and laying his hand on his head, he shall say:
'I anoint you with holy oil in the Lord, the Father Almighty and Christ Jesus and the Holy Spirit.'

And signing them on the forehead he shall kiss them saying:
'The Lord be with you;'
and he who is signed shall say:
'And with your spirit.'
And so he shall do to each one.
And immediately thereafter they shall pray with all the people. They shall not pray with the faithful until all these things are completed. And when they have prayed, they shall give the kiss of peace. (Hippolytus *Apostolic Tradition* 20-22)

The *Apostolic Tradition* is often quoted by scholars as proof of infant baptism in the earliest stage of the church. They usually refer to the statement which reads as follows: 'Then first baptize the little ones; those who can speak for themselves, shall do so; if not, their parents or some other relative shall speak for them.' These 'little ones' involved children who could speak for themselves, that is, who could respond to the questions of the bishop at the right moment using the prescribed words. Such children were surely not babies. Those who could not speak for themselves could be very young children who needed assistance in responding by pronouncing the required formulas. They were not exempted from the teaching and fasting preliminaries etc. The early Christian church never required a particular age for receiving baptism, and children who have accepted the faith and confessed their belief were indeed baptized. The question is not the fact that they were children, but whether this particular group who could not speak for themselves were indeed babies. One should then also assume that they could not partake in the whole ritual of baptism if they were indeed babies. However, one should also remember that the original Greek has not been recovered, except for a few small fragments. This quotation from the *Apostolic Tradition* is found in a Latin translation which dates from the fourth century. Some scholars have even suggested that it is not unlikely that this verse was inserted in the Latin translation since incidentally it was also in the fourth century that infant baptism became popular. If one decides to accept the expression 'little ones' as indeed referring to babies, then one should not apply this passage to situations before the fourth century since one must remember that the ancient translators had no objections to inserting and omitting phrases from the text from which they translated. They often adapted texts to suit their present situation. This can be clearly seen when one compares, for example, the extant sections of the Greek, Sahidic, Arabic, Ethiopic and Boharic translations of the *Apostolic Tradition*. (For a comparison of the different readings in these versions of the *Apostolic Tradition*, see Cuming 1976.)

The most important argument, however, for the later addition of this sentence is that it does not fit in very well in the whole pericope. As Aland (1963:43ff.) has pointed out, the sections which precede this baptismal regulation, deal exclusively with adult catechumens: their life is to be examined, their behaviour during their catechumenate is to be tested and they should spend the night which precedes their baptism in the reading of the Scriptures. These are all regulations which suit adult baptismal candidates, and definitely not infants. Aland concludes that it is very risky to base one's arguments for infant baptism on the statement that 'little ones too should be baptized'. He maintains that the rising popularity of infant baptism in the fourth century could have motivated a translator to insert a sentence to such an effect. He also refers to the Coptic translation having a statement that three years are required for a person to receive instruction in the Christian faith before baptism was administered.

But let us rather scrutinize the whole passage: Hippolytus tells us that the lives of those who were to be baptized were carefully examined. Thereafter they were daily exorcized. Though exorcism before baptism does not have a New Testament precedent, it is found in almost all the ancient baptismal liturgies. Hippolytus is possibly describing a baptismal ceremony which took place during Easter Weekend. Easter is one of the oldest feasts of the Christian church and was marked by special ceremonies, including baptism. The preparation for baptism started already on the Thursday when the catechumenates had to bathe themselves. On the Friday they fasted. The next day (Saturday) the final exorcism took place. The bishop then made a sign, perhaps the cross, on the forehead, ears and noses of the candidates. In order to prevent subsequent defilement, they spent the rest of the time, till their baptism, in the reading of the Scriptures.

The first act at the actual baptismal ceremony was the blessing of the water. If it were at all possible, the baptism had to take place in 'living' water (cf. the *Didache* chapter 2). Note that the baptismal candidates had to take off their clothes before they were baptized. We know from other writings that the taking off of clothes suggested the laying down of their earlier life. The reason for nudity in baptism is probably to fully expose the body, which had been exorcized, to the renewing influence of the water. This perhaps also explains why the women had to loosen their hair: it was merely to ensure that all the hair got wet. In fact, when a person was baptized, a sufficient quantity of water was used to properly wet the person. Sprinkling a few drops or even merely touching the head with moist fingers was a much later development. In fact, one can still find a few of the older churches in Europe today practising infant baptism and having a large enough baptismal font to receive the whole body of the infant. This is still a regular feature of infant baptism in the Greek Orthodox Church.

The anointing with oil before baptism derived from the ancient belief in the curative powers of oil (cf. Is. 5:14; Mk. 6:13). It appears that the bishop, who performed the actual baptism, was standing on the bank of the stream (or the edge of the font) while the deacon stood in the water to assist the baptismal candidate. From the earliest times the recitation of one or other form of a creed was linked to baptism. This was due to the requirement that candidates should confess their faith in Jesus before they could be baptized. A rudimentary form of such a creed at one of the first Christian baptisms can be found in some manuscripts (cf. Acts 8:37). In Acts 8:37 Philip baptized the eunuch after the latter had professed his faith as follows: 'I believe that Jesus Christ is the Son of God.' In the course of time more and more elements were added to this primitive form of the creed. However, after the introduction of infant baptism the creed ceased to be part of the baptismal liturgy.

To conclude: Hippolytus's *Apostolic Tradition* is an invaluable source of information concerning the practice of baptism in the first half of the third century. The regular practice was the baptism of adults having confessed their belief, but the text as we have it, also has a statement referring to very young children, probably also including infants. The Latin text is from the fourth century when infant baptism became a regular practice. If one insists however, that the Latin text does faithfully represent the lost Greek original, then one may say that in the third century the first traces of infant baptism occur, though the document still speaks of a fairly elaborate ceremony in which naturally only adults or older children could participate. If we accept this document as an early reference to infant baptism it is important to notice that the baptism of these infants was not linked to the covenant or the rite of circumcision. It was still an event following upon a verbal confession of faith.

CHAPTER 9

Origen

Origen was born of Christian parents about 185. His father Leonidas died as a martyr in the persecution of Severus. Origen fervently desired to join his father in martyrdom, but his mother prevented this by hiding his clothes. In 203, though only 18 years of age, he became the head of the school in Alexandria. Origen held this position until 231 and was very successful, but his growing reputation stirred the jealousy of Bishop Demetrius in Alexandria. The latter held synods in 231 and 232, and excommunicated Origen.

Origen went to Caesarea in Palestine and began the second part of his career. He again founded a school and continued his literary work. He died in 254, having suffered much torture during the Decian persecution.

Origen was an outstanding scholar of the early church and was widely respected by his contemporaries. He was a prolific author and many of his works have been preserved for us. More than a century after his death, however, he was anathematized by the church because of his doctrines. He nevertheless remains one of the greatest scholars of Christian antiquity.

There are three passages in Origen's writings which are frequently quoted in discussions on early references to infant baptism in the church of the first four centuries. Since these passages are very similar in contents, all three passages are cited before any comment is given:

Can a little one have committed sin? Yes, even though that young, he has sin, for which the sacrifice (of a pigeon) is commanded to be offered and from which even he who is but a day old is said not to be free of sin. Of this sin David is supposed to have said that which we cited earlier, 'In sin did my mother conceive me', for there is no mention in the history of any sin that his mother had committed. For this reason the Church received a tradition from the Apostles to give baptism even to infants. For the Apostles, to whom were entrusted the secrets of divine mysteries, knew that there is in everyone the inborn stains of sin, which must be washed away through water and the Spirit. (*Comm. on Rom.* v.9)

and

Every soul that is born into flesh is soiled by the filth of wickedness and sin. ... To these words it is possible to add, if we are requested to, the reason why baptism is given to the Church for the remission of sins; and according to the usage of the Church, baptism is given even to little children. And indeed if there were nothing in little children which required a remission of sins and thus nothing in them that pertained to forgiveness, the grace of baptism would seem superfluous. (*Hom. on Lev.* viii,2)

and

Little children were baptized 'for the remission of sins': for what sins? or when did they sin? Perhaps because 'no one is clean from pollution'; but this pollution is taken away by the mystery of baptism, and it is for this reason that little children are also baptized. (*Hom. on Lk.* xiv)

In these passages either the Greek term παιδία or the Latin term *parvuli* occurs. The Greek refers to children of all ages, from young to older teenagers, and may be employed to designate very young children if the context can help us to define the age of such children. The term itself is highly generic. The Latin term *parvuli* usually refers to relatively young children. In Greek these are usually signified by the term νήπιοι. It is only in Asterius the Sophist (chapter 16), that we find the Greek term βρέφη (which means 'infants' that is 'helpless babies') to refer to baptismal candidates. The Latin equivalent in this case would be *infants*, and occurs as such in Cyprian. In translating the passages from Origen that are quoted above, it would be better not to use the English term 'infant', but rather 'children' or 'young children'. To render all instances of παιδία, or νήπιοι, or *parvuli* merely by 'infant' would be begging the question.

In all three quotations Origen argues that even children need to be cleansed from sin and are accordingly baptized. Scholars who cite these passages to prove infant baptism as the *regular* baptismal practice in Origen's time fail to tell their readers what Origen's motivation was in his reference to the baptism of young children. Baptism for the remission of sins in Origen's writings cannot be equated with baptism as a sign of the covenant, since Origen's argument is not primarily a plea for infant baptism as a general rite, but a plea for remission of sins. Consequently, he refers to the fact that even children were baptized to make them pure - a practice also employed in the case of people who were on the point of death and should be allowed to depart without sin (see discussion in chapter 10).

The three passages above were all written towards the middle of the third century. It thus seems that these passages, as well as the *Apostolic Tradition* of Hippolytus and Cyprian's writings (cf. chapter 8 and chapter 13), prove that infant baptism, interpreted as a washing away of sins, began to appear in the third century. However, it was still not universally, nor even widely established, since there are too many writings in the third, fourth and fifth century which still bear evidence of so-called adult baptism though, in fact, adults as well as grown children were involved.

Origen's claim that they 'received a tradition from the Apostles to give baptism to children' and that 'according to the usage of the Church, baptism is given even to little children' needs more elucidation. These phrases were very popular among Church Fathers and they used them to defend many different doctrines. Often when they used the term 'apostolic tradition' they merely meant 'as the apostles handed it down to us in the Scriptures'. Thus the term was used in a way similar to the term 'scriptural' in our time. Today all the various religious groupings of people, no matter how divergent their beliefs, claim that they are 'scriptural', i.e. 'as the apostles handed it down to us in the Scriptures'.

Even if Origen did refer to a tradition or usage handed down to them, it is still extremely risky to accept his claim as such. How would we then explain all the statements about adult baptism which we have encountered in the previous chapters? Moreover, Justin too claims to be in accordance with the tradition of the church when he describes adult baptism (see p.34). This clearly shows that everybody laid claim to tradition when he/she wanted to substantiate any point of view.

However, the three passages quoted above have become so popular in modern literature that they overshadow other very interesting remarks of Origen on baptism. Let us look at some of his other statements which are seriously neglected. Origen also says:

> Let every one of the faithful recall the words he used in renouncing the devil when first he came to the waters of baptism, when he took upon himself the first seals of faith and came to the saving fountain: he proclaimed that he would not deal in the pomps of the devil, nor his works, nor would he submit to his servitude and his pleasures. (*Hom. on Num.* xii,4)

No doubt the passage above describes the baptism of a person who is mature enough to renounce the devil. But let us also look at the following passage:

These words follow: 'And all flesh shall see the salvation of God.' Since you were flesh, and you were indeed formerly flesh, and to speak more wonderfully, since you are even now in the flesh, you see the salvation of God. Concerning the words 'all flesh' – that nobody is saved who does not see the salvation of God – I leave this to be interpreted by these men who know how to examine the mysteries and the heart of the Scriptures. But this should be noted viz. that John speaks to people who have gone out to be baptized. If one wants to be baptized, he should go out; For he who remains in his original state and does not relinquish his habits and manners, he definitely does not come rightly to baptism. In order to understand what it means to go out to be baptized, receive the testimony and listen to the words which God speaks to Abraham: 'Leave your country' and what follows. And so John says the rest of the words to those people who are going out to be washed, not to those who have already gone out, but to those who are trying hard to go out. For if they have already gone out, he would not have said to them: 'Generation of vipers'. Thus that which he says to those people, he also says to you, o catechumens, ladies and men, who have decided to come to baptism. (*Hom. on Lk.* xxii,5-6)

There is no doubt that in this passage Origen expects baptismal candidates to renounce their sinful lives. If this condition is not complied with, baptism is wrongly administered, according to Origen.

Some very interesting conclusions can be drawn from the following section:

Those, then, who have followed the Saviour, and who have relinquished not a few things only, but rather all things, they will sit on twelve thrones and they will judge the twelve tribes of Israel. And they will receive this power at the resurrection of the dead. For this is a rebirth, it is a new birth, when the new heaven and the new earth are created for those who have renewed themselves and to whom is given a new covenant and the cup (of the new covenant). The prelude to this regeneration is that which is called by Paul 'the washing of regeneration'. The mystery of this newness is that which is brought about by the washing of the regeneration in the 'renewal of the Spirit'. Perhaps after birth nobody is clean from dirt, even if his life is one day, because of the mystery of the birth. Therefore David, as one of those who have gone through birth, says in the fiftieth Psalm that 'I was shapen in iniquity, and in sin did my mother conceive me.' And because of the regeneration of the washing, everybody who is born 'from above' 'in water and Spirit', will be clean from dirt, but if I can dare to say 'clean through a mirror' 'as in a riddle'. But at the other (second) rebirth, when the Son of Man will sit on his throne of glory, everyone who has come to that regeneration in Christ will be entirely clean from dirt and he will see 'face to face', and he will go to that rebirth through the washing of regeneration. But if you want to understand that washing, understand how John, who baptizes 'in water' for repentance says concerning the Saviour that 'He will baptize you in the Holy Spirit and in fire.' In the regeneration through washing we are buried with Christ. 'For we are buried with Him (according to the apostle) through baptism'. But through the regeneration of washing through fire and Spirit, we are conformed to 'the body of glory' of Christ who sits on the throne of his glory and we will sit on the twelve thrones, if we have left behind everything and have followed Christ. (*Comm. on Mt.* xv:22-23)

In the first place it is again very clear that Origen links baptism to the washing away of sins. Secondly, Origen says that 'those who have renewed themselves', have received the new covenant. Thus Origen regards repentance, and not baptism, as the new covenant. As a matter of fact, he explicitly says that the eucharist ('cup') is the sign of the new covenant, i.e. repentance. (Cf. also Mt. 26:28; Mk. 14:24; Lk. 22:20; 1 Cor. 11:25). He also explicitly says that baptism should be seen as the prelude to this new life. Thus at this stage the eucharist, and not baptism, is regarded as having come in the place of the old covenant (and circumcision).

It is important to recognize (from the above-quoted passages) that Origen refers to baptism as a rite administered to both adults and young children. In speaking of young children he explicitly says 'also' or 'even' to young children. It, therefore, seems plausible that in his time the first stage of the baptism of very young children could be assumed as having occurred along with the established practice of adult baptism. This, however, involved no problem at that stage since baptism was regarded as a rite that washes away sins and every person, irrespective of age, was full of sin.

In the next passage Origen gives a figurative interpretation of the crossing of the Red Sea. Just as the Israelites had to leave Egypt before they could cross the Red Sea, similarly the baptismal candidates should forsake the darkness of idolatry (their 'Egypt') and have a desire to listen to the divine law, before they can be baptized. By doing so they too can enter the restplaces of the desert and listen to the law of God and obey the precepts of the church. All these requirements seem to assume that the baptismal candidates were mature people. But let us cite Origen himself:

> Thus at the Jordan the ark of the Testament was the leader of the people of God. A body of priests and Levites stopped and as if from reverence for the ministers of God, the waters curbed their stream and piled up their water in a heap and gave a safe passage to the people of God. Do not be astonished that these things, which were done for an earlier nation, refer to you; to you, Christian,

who has crossed the Jordan stream through the sacrament of baptism. The divine Word promises you much greater and loftier things, namely a journey and a passage through the air itself. For listen to Paul who speaks about the just: 'We shall be caught up together in the clouds to meet the Lord in the air, and so shall we ever be with the Lord.' The just man, everyone who serves Him, has nothing to fear. Finally, listen to what God says when He promises him through the prophet: 'When you pass through fire, the flame will not burn you, for I am the Lord your God.' Thus every place receives the just man, and every creature will pay him due respect. Do not think that these things happened in earlier times, but that no such thing will happen to you who are now a hearer of these things. Everything will be fulfilled in you for a mystical reason. For you, who have lately forsaken the darkness of idolatry, and who desire to listen to the divine law, first of all abandon Egypt now. When you have joined the number of catechumens, and have begun to obey the precepts of the Church, you have crossed the Red Sea. You have placed yourself in the restplaces of the desert and everyday you have the opportunity to listen to the law of God and to look at the countenance of Moses which is revealed through the glory of God. If indeed, you will have come to the mystical fountain of baptism and will be initiated, in the presence of priests and Levites, in those venerable and magnificent sacraments, which are known by those who are allowed to know, then you also, through the ministries of the priests, will cross the Jordan and enter the land of promise, in which, after Moses, Jesus now receives you, and He Himself becomes the leader of your new journey. If you indeed remember the many and great virtues of God that He has divided the sea for you, and that the water of the river came to a standstill, you will turn to them and say: 'What ails you, o sea, that you flee, and you, Jordan, that you turn back? O mountains, that you skip like rams? O hills, like lambs?' But the divine Word will answer you and say: 'Tremble, o earth, at the presence of the Lord, at the presence of the God of Jacob, who turns the rock into a pool of water, the cliff into a spring of water.' (*Hom. on Joshua*, 4,1)

To conclude, Origen provides us with some very interesting insights into the practice and theology of baptism in the church of the third century. Though he refers to adults, or at least grown children, as the subjects of the rite of baptism, Origen nevertheless acknowledges the occasional participation of infants. That is to say, that one may regard Origen as one of the first authors who explicitly mentions the involvement of infants. However, one must be careful not to assume that infant baptism was a widely established practice in his day. As in the case of the *Apostolic Tradition* (chapter 8) the first occurrences of infant baptism may be noted at this time. It is important to weigh all the evidence and to bear in mind that the inception of infant baptism was probably a slow process, since subsequent authors mentioned in the following chapters provide us with overwhelming evidence for believer's baptism (whether adults or young children) as the more general practice. It is also important to realize that there was, strictly speaking, no such thing as a unified early church. While a particular practice developed in one area of the ancient world (and for that matter, the ancient Christian church) an older custom may have continued long thereafter in other areas. All we can say justifiably is that during the third and fourth centuries infant baptism began to occur and increased gradually.

Another important observation which has to be linked to the above is the so-called clinical baptism (see chapter 10). It could well be that Origen's 'even' refers to this custom. If so, Origen's remarks are not to be taken as a major shift, but rather as an additional allowance. Consequently one could say little more than that in Origen's time the first occurrences are acknowledged, though they would not have been regarded as the general practice, since the reasons for the baptizing of these infants were not new theological insights, but rather a concession to accommodate special cases. This explains Origen's 'we even baptize infants' in a more satisfactory way.

CHAPTER 10

Christian tomb inscriptions

During the third and fourth century a fairly large number of Christian tombstone inscriptions became important witnesses to the practice of infant baptism in the early church. These inscriptions, some in Greek, some in Latin, have received considerable attention in the debate on the origin of infant baptism. The Latin inscriptions are by far the majority and are well known from the edition of E. Diehl, *Inscriptiones latinae christianae veteres*, Berlin 1961. The Greek inscriptions can be found in J.C. Didier, *Le baptême des enfants dans la tradition de l'église*, Monumenta Christiana Selecta VII, Tournai 1959. The best account of the nature and relevance of these inscriptions was given by Everett Ferguson, 'Inscriptions and the origin of infant baptism' in *The Journal of Theological Studies*, 1979, pp. 37-46.

It is noteworthy that the Christian tombstone inscriptions use various terms referring to baptism, such as 'being made a believer' or merely 'believer' or even 'died in peace', 'received grace', 'became a neophyte', etc. The ages of the deceased are also very remarkable. These vary greatly from very young children to quite elderly people with a large variety in between. What is important is the fact that these baptisms occurred shortly before death and probably refer to what Ferguson called 'emergency baptism' in the case of imminent death to ensure that they may go to heaven according to the theology at the time. In the case of very young children these inscriptions do give evidence to the fact that in the third and fourth centuries infants were also baptized. However, these instances do not pertain to a general practice of infant baptisms but rather to a peculiar method of safeguarding a person's eternal future.

Let us now consider the actual wording on the relevant stones illustrating the baptism of young children, as cited by Ferguson:

(1) ... obtained (the grace) of God on December 5 and lived in this world after the day of obtaining until December 7 and died ...

(2) Here is laid Fortunia, who lived more or less 4 years. The parents set this up for their dearest daughter. She obtained (grace) on July 25 ... and died on July 27.

Both these died two days after having been baptized. In the case of example 2 the child was four years old. There are many examples such as these, illustrating a baptism almost on the deathbed. This is stated explicitly in the following:

(3) Her parents set this up for Julia Florentina, their dearest and most innocent infant who was made a believer. She was born a pagan on the day before the nones of March before dawn when Zoilus was censor of the province. She lived eighteen months and twenty-two days and was made a believer in the eighth hour of the night, almost drawing her last breath.

(4) Sacred to the divine dead. Florentius made this monument for his well-deserving son Appronianus, who lived one year, nine months, and five days. Since he was dearly loved by his grandmother, and she saw that he was going to die, she asked from the church that he might depart from the world a believer.

(5) Pastor, Titiana, Marciana, and Chreste made this for Marcianus, a well-deserving son in Christ the Lord. He lived 12 years, 2 months, and ... days. He received grace on September 20 when the consuls were Marinianus and Paternus the second time. He gave up (his soul) on September 21. May you live among the saints in eternity.

(6) Postumius Eutenion, a believer, who obtained holy grace the day before his birthday at a very late hour and died.

(7) Sweet Tyche lived one year, 10 months, 15 days. Received (grace) on the 8th day before the Kalends ... Gave up (her soul) on the same day.

(8) Irene who lived with her parents 10 months and 6 days received (grace) on April 7 and gave up (her soul) on April 13.

In the following inscriptions (nrs. 9-14) the term 'neophyte' applies to persons who were new Christians and therefore also newly baptized. Some of these were young children, but others were adults. In all these cases it could be said that the persons involved probably died shortly after having become believers, since they are explicitly called 'neophytes'. The prevalent theological view of the third and fourth centuries that baptism was necessary in order to go to heaven and therefore an important preparation for the after-life could, in the case of explicitly mentioned neophytes, explain these examples as baptisms administered to persons in danger of death. Note the following inscriptions:

(9) Aristo, an innocent child, who lived 8 months a neophyte, departed on June 4, Timasius and Promotus being consuls.
(10) Innocentius a neophyte lived 23 years.
(11) For Paulinus, a neophyte, in peace, who lived 8 years.

(12) For Proiectus, an infant neophyte, who lived 2 years, 7 months.
(13) Mercury a neophyte is buried here. He lived 42 years, 2 months, 15 days.
(14) For the well-deserving Eugenia a happy memory who lived not 19 years, a neophyte.

The doctrine of inherited original sin, which became popular in the third and fourth centuries, tied in well with baptism symbolizing the washing away of sins. In the chapters on Origen (chapter 9) and Cyprian (chapter 13) it is shown how the problem of baptizing infants was addressed. Since it could hardly be said of infants that they committed sin, how could they be baptized? This problem was related to baptism as a preparation for the after-life and thus the two doctrines ('inherited sin' and 'preparing for heaven') reinforced each other in validating the necessity of baptizing people when very ill and in danger of death. Ferguson (quoted above) shows how this is often referred to as 'emergency baptism' or 'clinical baptism'. The instances of young children and even infants having been baptized shortly before they died, as shown by the Christian tombstone inscriptions, also do not validate a general practice of infant baptism in the third and fourth centuries, since at that time there was pressure for delaying baptism in order to go to heaven with a clean record. These tombstone inscriptions show how strong the notion was of baptism as a necessity for entrance into the next world.[1] Therefore, very young children and even infants were baptized in cases of imminent death. On the other hand, the theological views as well as the custom of emergency baptism paved the way for renewed considerations

---

[1] Origen in his *Homily on Luke* (xiv, 5) quotes John 3:5 'unless one is born of water and the Spirit he cannot enter the kingdom of heaven'. Origen wrote in the context of the idea of original sin being removed by baptism and he therefore understood the phrase 'born of water' as referring to baptism, instead of to 'natural birth' in contrast to 'spiritual birth', which is the issue in John 3:5 as is clearly stated in John 3:6.

in the early church of the significance of baptism. As such these developments made it all the more acceptable to baptize infants and can be seen as part of the changed situation, in which infant baptism gradually came to be more generally practised from the fourth century onwards.

CHAPTER 11

The Teaching of the Apostles (Didascalia Apostolorum)

The Teaching of the Apostles (Didascalia Apostolorum) is a collection of miscellaneous precepts. It was composed in the earlier half of the third century for a community of Christian converts in the northern part of Syria. The unknown compiler of this work seems to have been a Jew by birth. Except for a few small fragments, the original Greek text has been lost. Fortunately the *Didascalia* has been preserved in its entirety in a Syriac translation while substantial portions of a Latin version also survived.

The *Didascalia* provides us with important information concerning the rite of baptism in the Syrian Church in the third century. In this source we read, for example, the following:

> In the first place, when women descend into the water, those who descend into the water should be anointed by a deaconess with the oil of anointing; and when there is no woman present, and especially no deaconess, he who baptizes must of necessity anoint her who is being baptized. But when there is a woman present, and especially a deaconess, it is not becoming that women should be seen by men: but with the laying on of hands you must anoint the head only. As of old the priests and kings were anointed in Israel, you must do in like manner, with the laying on of hands, anoint the head of those who receive

baptism, whether of men or of women; and afterwards - whether you yourself baptize, or you order the deacons or presbyters to baptize - let a woman deacon, as we have already said, anoint the women. But let a man pronounce over them the invocation of the divine Names in the water. And when she who is being baptized has ascended from the water, let the deaconess receive her, and teach and instruct her how the seal of baptism should be kept unbroken in purity and holiness. For this reason we say that the ministry of a woman deacon is especially needful and important. For our Lord and Saviour also was ministered unto by women ministers, Mary Magdalene, and Mary the daughter of James and mother of Joseph and the mother of the sons of Zebedee, with other women beside. (*Didascalia* 16 (iii.12))

From the above we can identify different elements of the baptismal rite in the Syrian Church. The pre-baptismal acts consisted of the anointing of the baptismal candidate as well as the imposition of hands. It is not clear from this passage whether there were two anointings – an anointing of the head and an anointing of the whole body. The latter is suggested by the remark that women should be used to anoint women since 'it is not fitting that women should be seen by men'. It is often stated that the *Didascalia* is a diffuse document and that the author had limited literary gifts. Thus the obscurity of the exact meaning of this passage should be seen in this light. Nevertheless, women, preferably but not necessarily deaconesses, were used to anoint women who were to be baptized.

The *Didascalia* does not describe any post-baptismal anointing such as we find in Tertullian, Hippolytus, Cyprian, Cyril of Jerusalem and the *Apostolic Constitutions.* As a matter of fact the usual post-baptismal acts (viz. the anointing and the imposition of hands) here precede the baptism. This description is in line with other accounts of baptismal ceremonies in the Syrian Church of the third century.

It is very interesting to note that the author also tells us that bishops could also ask the *deacon* or *presbyters* to baptize the candidates. Women, however, were not allowed to perform this sacramental act since the invocation of the trinitarian formula could be pronounced by men only.

At another place in this same work it is again stated that women were not allowed to administer baptism. Though the reason given may seem far-fetched, the passage shows how this requirement was justified:

> That a woman should baptize, or that one should be baptized by a woman, we do not advise, for it is a transgression of the commandment, and a great danger to her who baptizes and to him who is baptized. For if it were lawful to be baptized by a woman, our Lord and Teacher Himself would have been baptized by Mary His mother, whereas He was baptized by John, like other people. Do not therefore endanger yourselves, brothers and sisters, by acting contrary to the law of the Gospel. (*Didascalia* 15)

It is generally admitted that the author of the *Didascalia* was not a theologian and that he showed little interest in doctrinal matters. He is nevertheless in line with contemporary theologians when he too links baptism to the forgiveness of sins:

> But again, by baptism the sins are forgiven of those who from the Gentiles come near and enter the holy Church of God ... Let us hear then, brothers, for the Scripture says: Who shall boast himself and say: I am free of sins? Or who shall be confident and say: I am innocent? And again: There is no man pure of defilement: even though his life is only but one day. To every one therefore who believes and is baptized his former sins have been forgiven; but after baptism also it is forgiven, provided that he has not committed a deadly sin nor been an accomplice thereto, but has only heard, or seen

sin, or spoken about it, and thus may be seen as guilty of sin. But if a man go forth from the world by martyrdom for the name of the Lord, blessed is he; for brothers who by martyrdom have gone forth from this world, of these the sins are covered. (*Didascalia* 20)

In the above passage the author also touches upon post-baptismal sin. It appears that he believes that baptism can wash away even post-baptismal sins, provided that a deadly sin has not been committed. There were people in the church of the third century who believed that if Christians sinned after baptism, they would not again obtain forgiveness. This author, however, displayed more leniency in his views on post-baptismal sins. Together with other writers, he also believes that martyrdom, which was often called 'the baptism of blood', could redeem someone from every sin. Nevertheless, there are other passages in this same work where the author seems to argue that those who sin after their baptism could not again obtain remission of their sins:

But if, after baptism, a man should corrupt and defile the wife of another man, or be polluted with a harlot, and he should, rising up from her, bathe in all the seas and oceans and be baptized in all the rivers, he cannot be made clean. (*Didascalia* 26)

and

For we believe not, brothers, that when a man has once descended into the water he will do again the abominable and filthy works of the ungodly heathen. For this is clear and known to all, that whosoever does evil after baptism, such a person is already condemned to the Gehenna of fire. (*Didascalia* 5)

The above two passages, however, should not be interpreted as if the author denies post-baptismal repentance. This would contradict the other explicit references in this work to penance after baptism. It rather appears that the author is merely emphasizing in hyperbolic terms the need to lead a holy life after baptism. He believes that the Holy Spirit is conferred at baptism upon the candidate. Thereafter the Holy Spirit will remain with this person and this will oblige the person to lead a holy life. This may be deduced from the following passage:

> For through baptism they receive the Holy Spirit, who is always with those who do what is right and does not depart from them because of natural issues and the intercourse of marriage, but is ever and always with those who possess Him, and keeps them... (*Didascalia* 26)

The same idea is also found in the next passage:

> 'For the unclean spirit, when he has gone out from a man, departs and goes about in waterless places' - that is, men who do not descend into the water of baptism - 'and when he has found no rest, he said: I will return to my former house, for where I came out....' Learn now, why, when the unclean spirit has gone out, he finds no rest in any place: because every man whosoever is filled with a spirit, one with the Holy Spirit, and another with an unclean spirit. A believer is filled with the Holy Spirit, and an unbeliever with an unclean spirit: and his nature does not receive a foreign spirit. He therefore who has withdrawn and separated himself and departed from the unclean spirit by baptism, is filled with the Holy Spirit; and if he do good works, the Holy Spirit stays with him, and he remains fulfilled; and the unclean spirit finds no place in him, for he who is filled with the Holy Spirit does not receive him... (*Didascalia* 26)

In the following passage the author of the *Didascalia* makes a very interesting statement when he says:

> And as for baptism also, one baptism is enough for you, since one baptism has perfectly forgiven you your sins. For Isaiah said not only 'Wash', but 'Wash, and be cleansed'. (*Didascalia* 24)

The author here says that it is unnecessary to be baptized more than once. One should not, however, apply this statement in a manner similar to modern-day examples of rebaptism. The above statement should be understood in terms of the meaning baptism had for these early Christians. They believed that baptism washed away the sins of men. As such, then, it was unnecessary (note his words: 'one is enough') to be baptized anew because there would be no need thereof after the washing away of all the sins at one's first baptism, since this washing also provided for future sins as has been shown in the passages above. Rebaptism, therefore, would not make any difference.

CHAPTER 12

Novatian

Our information about Novatian is scanty and is derived from the works of his adversaries. One can naturally suspect that their statements are tinged with prejudice. Nevertheless, what is known about his life provides us with remarkable information regarding current opinions on baptism in his time. He must have been born about 190-120 and he probably died as a martyr under Valerian in 257-8. Before Novatian's conversion, he was a Stoic philosopher. Novatian hoped to become bishop of Rome and was very disappointed when Cornelius was elected in 251. He then set himself up as anti-pope and he became a leader of a rival group, called Novatianism, which advocated a rigorous position with regard to the lapsed (= those who apostatized during persecution but who, after the persecution ended, wanted to be readmitted to the church).

Cornelius, bishop of Rome from 251-3, gives us interesting information concerning Novatian's baptism. A particularly interesting fact about his life and career is found in Eusebius's quotation of a passage from Cornelius, who defended the rejection of Novatian as pope. He writes:

> Permit us to say further: On account of what works or conduct had he (= Novatian) the assurance to contend for the episcopate? Was it that he had been brought up in the Church from the beginning, and had endured many conflicts on her behalf, and had passed through many and great dangers for religion? Truly this is not the fact.

But Satan, who entered and dwelt in him for a long time, became the occasion of his believing. Being delivered by the exorcists, he fell into a severe sickness; and as he seemed about to die, he received baptism by affusion, on the bed where he lay; if indeed we can say that such a one did receive it. And when he was healed of his sickness he did not receive the other things which it is necessary to have according to the canon of the Church, even the being sealed by the bishop. And as he did not receive this, how could he receive the Holy Spirit? (Eusebius in his *Ecclesiastical History* vi,xliii,13-5)

It is clear from the section quoted above that clinical baptism, administered by effusion, was regarded as an inferior baptism. Moreover, Novatian's own writings show how he, as all other theologians of the third century, linked baptism to the remission of sins, but never to circumcision:

Because, when it is written that 'flesh and blood do not inherit the kingdom of God,' it is not the substance of the flesh that is condemned, which was built up by the divine hands that it should not perish, but only the guilt of the flesh is rightly rebuked, which by the voluntary daring of man rebelled against the claims of divine law. Because of baptism and in the dissolution of death the flesh is raised up and returns to salvation, by being recalled to the condition of innocence when the mortality of guilt is put away. (*The Trinity* 10,9)

Since baptism was linked to the remission of sins and consequently salvation, it was regarded as a *second birth*. This concurs with the idea that baptism had regenerative power, as stated above. Novatian, for example, continues as follows:

He (= the Holy Spirit) it is who effects with water the second birth, as a certain seed of divine generation, and a consecration of a heavenly nativity, the pledge of a promised inheritance, and as it were a kind of handwriting of eternal salvation. (*The Trinity* 29,16)

The concept of baptism as a 'rebirth' is found in another work of Novatian as well:

You know that you are the temple of the Lord, the members of Christ, the dwelling place of the Holy Ghost, elected to hope, consecrated to the faith destined for salvation, sons of God, brothers of Christ, and associates of the Holy Spirit, owing nothing any longer to the flesh **because you have been reborn of water**. (*In Praise of Purity* 2,1)

Though Novatian does not give us explicit information on the rite of baptism, his life and writings give us important insights into the theology of baptism. Of special importance are the remarks that baptism entails a rebirth, the washing away of sins, and the bestowing of the Holy Spirit. In the case of Novatian's own baptism the fact that he received it by affusion, raised questions as to the validity of the blessings associated with baptism.

CHAPTER 13

Cyprian

Cyprian was born of pagan parents in Africa (probably Carthage) between 200 and 210. He was, before his conversion, a man of wealth and good social position. In about 246 Cyprian was converted to Christianity. He sold his estates and gave his money to the poor. At his baptism he adopted the name of Caecilius, the person who played a major role in his conversion.

In 248 or 249 Cyprian was elected bishop of Carthage. When the Decian persecution broke out in 250, he decided to go into hiding and direct his congregation by writing letters to his church. Nevertheless his flight surprised many people and he later had to defend this decision. In 251 he returned to Carthage. The question of the treatment of the lapsed caused much dissension and led to the formation of another schismatic group, headed by Novatian and Felicissimus. They and their adherents were then banned by Cyprian. A new controversy, concerning rebaptism, arose in Cyprian's church but was put to a stop by a new persecution under the Emperor Valerian. Cyprian was beheaded during this persecution in 257.

Cyprian is the first Church Father who bears indubitable witness to the practice of infant baptism in the Christian church of the third century. According to Everett Ferguson (1979:37), Africa was probably the area in which infant baptism found its earliest and most widespread acceptance. In a reply to a question of Fidus, an African bishop, Cyprian sent a letter to inform him of the decision of the council. Cyprian wrote as follows in 253:

2. But in respect of the case of the infants, which you say ought not to be baptized within the second or third day after their birth, and that the law of ancient circumcision should be regarded, so that you think that one who is just born should not be baptized and sanctified within the eighth day, we all thought very differently in our council. For in this course which you thought was to be taken, no one agreed; but we all rather judge that the mercy and grace of God is not to be refused to any one born of man. For as the Lord says in His Gospel, 'The Son of man is not come to destroy men's lives, but to save them,' as far as we can, we must strive that, if possible, no soul be lost. For what is lacking to him who has once been formed in the womb by the hands of God? To us, indeed, and to our eyes, those who are newly born seem to receive the increase according to the worldly course of days. As for the rest, whatever things have been made by God, have been perfected by the majesty and work of God, the Maker.

3. Moreover, belief in divine Scripture declares to us, that among all, whether infants or those who are older, there is the same equality of the divine gift. Elisha, beseeching God, so laid himself upon the infant son of the widow, who was lying dead, that his head was applied to his head, and his face to his face, and the limbs of Elisha were spread over and joined to each of the limbs of the child, and his feet to his feet. If this thing be considered with respect to the inequality of our birth and our body, an infant could not be made equal with a person grown up and mature, nor could its little limbs fit and be equal to the larger limbs of a man. But in that is expressed the divine and spiritual equality, that all men are alike and equal, since they have once been made by God; and our age may have a difference in the increase of our bodies, according to the world, but not according to God; unless that very grace also which is given to the baptized is given

either less or more, according to the age of the receivers, whereas the Holy Spirit is not given with measure, but by the love and mercy of the Father alike to all. For God, as He does not accept the person, so He does not accept the age; since He shows Himself a Father to all with well-weighed equality for the attainment of heavenly grace.

4. For, with respect to what you say, that the aspect of an infant in the first days after its birth is not pure, so that any one of us would still shudder at kissing it, we do not think that this ought to be alleged as any impediment to heavenly grace. For it is written, 'To the pure all things are pure.' Nor ought any of us to shudder at that which God has condescended to make. For although the infant is still fresh from its birth, yet it is not such that any one should shudder at kissing it in giving grace and in making peace; since in the kiss of an infant every one of us ought, for his very religion's sake, to consider the still recent hands of God themselves, which in some sort we are kissing, in the man lately formed and freshly born, when we are embracing that which God has made. For in respect of the observance of the eighth day in the Jewish circumcision of the flesh, a sacrament was given beforehand in shadow and in usage; but when Christ came, it was fulfilled in truth. For because the eighth day, that is, the first day after the Sabbath, was to be that on which the Lord should rise again, and should quicken us, and give us circumcision of the spirit, the eighth day, that is, the first day after the Sabbath, and the Lord's day, went before in the figure; which figure ceased when by and by the truth came, and spiritual circumcision was given to us.

5. For which reason we think that no one is to be hindered from obtaining grace by that law which was already ordained, and that spiritual circumcision ought not to be hindered by carnal circumcision, but that absolutely every man is to be admitted to the grace of Christ, since Peter also in the Acts of the Apostles speaks, and

says, 'The Lord has said to me that I should call no man common or unclean.' But if anything could hinder men from obtaining grace, their more heinous sins might rather hinder those who are mature and grown up and older. But again, if even to the greatest sinners, and to those who had sinned much against God, when they subsequently believed, remission of sins is granted – and nobody is hindered from baptism and from grace – how much rather ought we to shrink from hindering an infant, who, being lately born, has not sinned, except in that, being born after the flesh according to Adam, he has contracted the contagion of the ancient death at its earliest birth, who approaches the more easily on this very account to the reception of the forgiveness of sins – that to him are remitted, not his own sins, but the sins of another.

6. And therefore, dearest brother, this was our opinion in council, that by us no one ought to be hindered from baptism and from the grace of God, who is merciful and kind and loving to all. Which, since it is to be observed and maintained in respect of all, we think it to be even more observed in respect of infants and newly-born persons, who on this very account deserve more from our help and from the divine mercy, that immediately, on the very beginning of their birth, lamenting and weeping, they do nothing else but entreat. We bid you, dearest brother, ever heartily farewell. (*Epistle* 58; *al.* 64)

Note, that Cyprian does argue for infant baptism, but not on the grounds of the covenant or of circumcision. As a matter of fact, he dissociates himself from the rite of circumcision by ordering Fidus not to delay baptism till the eighth day. It is also important to note that Fidus, on the other hand, preferred to wait till the eighth day not because he believed that circumcision was replaced by baptism, but because he thought that children in the first days after their birth were too repulsive to give them the kiss of peace. Thus Fidus's appeal to circumcision was not based on any supposed theological link between baptism and circumcision. He merely used a form of argumentation which was very popular in ancient times and which was called 'analogy'. The Church Fathers would argue, for example, on the basis of analogy, that the waning and waxing of the moon would prove the resurrection of man in the last days. But this would not mean that they saw any theological connection between the moon and resurrection. However, the analogy probably became the starting-point of associating infant baptism with the rite of circumcision. One should be very careful not to conclude that it was a generally accepted doctrine since even in Augustine's day (4th/5th century) the relating of infant baptism to circumcision was not a dogmatic issue at all, but rather an analogy which gradually developed into a formal dogma. Circumcision at first, as in Cyprian's argument above, is applied to the time of baptism (8th day) which Cyprian himself contested. The main contention of infant baptism, however, is clearly shown by Cyprian's argument that God's grace, i.e. his salvation, should be open and free to all. As such it could not be denied to anyone. Infants had the same right as any other person to be initiated into the body of believers. This was in line with the ancient thinking about baptism, namely, that baptism actually washes away sin and grants the recipient entrance into heaven. As such baptism would have had salvation power.

Cyprian also believed that the church (in fact, *his* church) was sanctioned to administer baptism, remission of sins, and thus by implication salvation. This is illustrated by another letter of Cyprian, written in the year 255, and addressed to Magnus, an African Christian, in which he gives us more information concerning his views on baptism:

> With your usual religious diligence, you have consulted my poor intelligence, dearest son, as to whether, among other heretics, they also who come from Novatian ought, after his profane washing, to be baptized, and sanctified

in the Catholic Church, with the lawful, and true, and only baptism of the Church. Respecting which matter, as much as the capacity of my faith and the sanctity and truth of the divine Scriptures suggest, I answer, that no heretics and schismatics at all have any power or right. For which reason Novatian neither ought to be nor can be made an exception because he himself, abiding outside of the Church and acting in opposition to the peace and love of Christ, should be considered among adversaries and antichrists .... Peter also, showing this, set forth that the Church is one, and that only they who are in the Church can be baptized; and said, 'In the ark of Noah, few, that is, eight souls, were saved by water; the like figure whereunto even baptism shall save you:' proving and attesting that the one ark of Noah was a type of the one Church. If, then, in that baptism of the world thus expiated and purified, he who was not in the ark of Noah could be saved by water, he who is not in the Church to which alone baptism is granted, can also now be quickened by baptism .... But if the Church is one which is loved by Christ, and is alone cleansed by His washing, how can he who is not in the Church be either loved by Christ, or washed and cleansed by His washing?

3. Wherefore, since the Church alone has the living water, and the power of baptizing and cleansing man, he who says that any one can be baptized and sanctified by Novatian must first show and teach that Novatian is in the Church, or presides over the Church ... nor ought it to trouble any one that sick people seem to be sprinkled or affused, when they obtain the Lord's grace, when Holy Scripture speaks by the mouth of the prophet Ezekiel, and says, 'Then will I sprinkle clean water upon you, and you shall be clean: from all your filthiness and from all your idols will I cleanse you. And I will give you a new heart, and a new spirit will I put within you.' Also in Numbers: 'And the man that shall be unclean until the

evening shall be purified on the third day, and on the seventh day shall be clean: but if he shall not be purified on the third day, on the seventh day he shall not be clean. And that soul shall be cut off from Israel: because the water of sprinkling has not been sprinkled upon him.' And again: 'And the Lord spoke unto Moses, saying, Take the Levites from among the children of Israel, and cleanse them. And thus should you do unto them, to cleanse them: you should sprinkle them with the water of purification.' And again: 'The water of sprinkling is a purification.' Whence it appears that the sprinkling also of water prevails equally with the washing of salvation; and that when this is done in the Church, where the faith both of receiver and giver is sound, all things hold and may be consummated and perfected by the majesty of the Lord and by the truth of faith ... And therefore, as far as it is allowed me by faith to conceive and to think, this is my opinion, that any one should be esteemed a legitimate Christian, who by the law and right of faith shall have obtained the grace of God in the Church. Or if any one think that those have gained nothing from this because they have been only sprinkled by the life-giving water, but that they are still empty and void, let them not be deceived, so as if they overcome the inconvenience of their sickness and become well, they should seek to be baptized ... Unless, indeed, it seems just to some, that they who are polluted among adversaries and antichrists by profane water outside the Church should be considered baptized; while they who are baptized in the Church seem to have gained less of divine mercy and grace; and so great honour should be considered for the heretics that, when they come, they should not be questioned as to whether they were bathed or sprinkled, whether they were patient or peripatetic; but among us the sound truth of faith is disparaged, and in ecclesiastical baptism its majesty and sanctity suffer derogation. (*Epistle* 75; *al.* 69)

In the first place, it is clear from the above quoted passage that Cyprian attributes the same meaning to baptism as all the other Church Fathers whom we have discussed, though he differed from them by advocating infant baptism. Cyprian, too, regards baptism as 'washing away' of sins, and thus as a 'cleansing' or 'purification' of the baptismal candidate. In the preceding chapters we saw how this belief prompted the early Christians to delay their baptism till a sickbed or a period of time when death was imminent. This same belief had the opposite effect in Cyprian's theology. He and his council decided to administer baptism in the beginning of someone's life, rather than postponing it until the latter part of his life. The covenant played no role in their reasoning. The basic contention of their theology was that everyone, irrespective of age, was entitled to God's grace.

It is also clear from this section that immersion was still the normal practice in Cyprian's time. This caused many early Christians to argue that those (in fact, the sick) who received clinical baptism 'have gained nothing from this because they have been only sprinkled by the life-giving water.' They even argued that such people should be rebaptized when 'they overcome the inconvenience of their sickness and become well'. Cyprian therefore deemed it necessary to counter this belief and he argued that those who were sprinkled were still legitimate Christians and did not receive less grace. This objection to sprinkling, raised by other early Christians, reminds us of the section in Novatian where we read that clinical baptism administered by sprinkling was inferior and that those who received this baptism were possibly even debarred from ordination.

Cyprian is our first clear witness for using the term sprinkle (Latin: *aspergo*) which probably referred to a proper sprinkling of water on the sick person, not a mere wetting with a few drops. However, it is noteworthy that even for Cyprian the amount of water was not decisive since he uses the phrase 'aspergo vel profundi', i.e. clearly showing whether one sprinkles or drenches properly does not make any difference to the validity of the rite. He probably emphasized this fact to counteract the views of other ancient theologians who acknowledged only a proper immersion as a real baptism.

We should remember that Cyprian's view of baptism was not shared by all other churches of his time. The main thrust of Cyprian's argument in the letter above, for example, deals with the question of rebaptism. Cyprian believed that those who were baptized by schismatic and heretic groups should be rebaptized when they return to the orthodox church. This view was strongly opposed by the church of the West who admitted to the orthodox church even persons baptized in heretic groups by mere imposition of hands. When the decisions of Cyprian, confirmed by two Councils at Carthage in 255 and 256, were submitted to Pope Stephen I, he refused to sanction rebaptism and he threatened the African bishops with excommunication if they continued the practice. This controversy came to an end after the deaths of Stephen (257) and Cyprian (258) and after a new outbreak of persecutions.

Cyprian discusses the issue of rebaptism in another letter which he wrote in 255:

> 1. When we were together in council, dearest brethren, we read your letter which you wrote to us concerning those who seem to be baptized by heretics and schismatics, (asking) whether, when they come to the Catholic Church, which is one, they ought to be baptized. On which matter, although you yourselves hold thereupon the truth and certainty of the Catholic rule, yet since you have thought that of our mutual love we ought to be consulted, we put forward our opinion, not as a new one, but we join with you in equal agreement, in an opinion long since decreed by our predecessors, and observed by us, – judging, namely, and holding it for certain that no one can be baptized abroad outside the Church, since there is one baptism appointed in the holy Church. And it is written in the words of the Lord, 'They have forsaken me,

the fountain of living waters, and hewed them out broken cisterns, which can hold no waters.' And again, sacred Scripture warns, and says, 'Reform from the strange water, and drink not from a fountain of strange water.' (*Epistle* 69; *al.* 70)

In a letter which Cyprian wrote in 255 and which he addressed to Quintus of Mauretania, an African bishop, he admits that his point of view was not held by all other theologians of his time:

(1) ... But again some of our colleagues would rather give honour to heretics than agree with us; and while by the assertion of one baptism they are unwilling to baptize those that come, they thus either themselves make two baptisms in saying that there is a baptism among heretics; or certainly, which is a matter of more importance, they strive to set before and prefer the sordid and profane washing of heretics to the true and only and legitimate baptism of the Catholic Church, not considering that it is written, 'He who is baptized by one dead, of what avail is his washing?' (*Epistle* 70; *al.* 71)

Cyprian also believed that it was not necessary to rebaptize Christians who were baptized in the orthodox church, but thereafter strayed to heretic groups, and eventually returned to the orthodox church again:

(2) ... Which also we observe in the present day, that it is sufficient to lay hands for repentance upon those who are known to have been baptized in the Church, and have gone over from us to the heretics, if, subsequently acknowledging their sin and putting away their error, they return to the truth and to their parent; so that, because it had been a sheep, the Shepherd may receive into His fold the estranged and vagrant sheep. (*Epistle* 70; *al.* 71)

Cyprian

We know that some schismatic groups also rebaptized Christians who joined them and who had been baptized by the orthodox church. Cyprian mentions this in a letter which he wrote in 256 to Jubaian, a Mauretanian bishop. Cyprian was very adamant and even compared Novatian, the leader of a schismatic group, to a monkey:

> 2. Nor does what you have described in your letters disturb us, dearest brother, that the Novatians rebaptize those whom they entice from us, since it does not in any wise matter to us what the enemies of the Church do, so long as we ourselves hold a regard for our power, and the steadfastness of reason and truth. For Novatian, after the manner of apes - which, although they are not men, yet imitate human doings - wishes to claim to himself the authority and truth of the Catholic Church, while he himself is not in the Church; nay, moreover, has stood forth hitherto as a rebel and enemy against the Church. For, knowing that there is one baptism, he arrogates to himself this one, so that he may say that the Church is with him, and make us heretics. (*Epistle* 72; *al.* 73)

It is noteworthy that the point of contention between these schismatic groups was not the fact that the persons baptized were requested to confess their belief, but rather that they were baptized in the proper way. Therefore it was not a matter of content but of manner. This is in line with the thinking of the time namely, that baptism makes one a believer, and therefore the correct form of baptism should be observed. As such we are to note a significant shift in theology: 'baptism causes belief' instead of 'baptism symbolizes belief' as was the opinion among the earliest Church Fathers.

To conclude: Cyprian does tell us about infant baptism in the third century in North Africa, but, as we have seen above, we should not interpret Cyprian's point of view as being representative of all the churches in the regions where Christianity flourished. Nevertheless, Cyprian's church is an important witness to the early stages of infant baptism and to a time of controversy until infant baptism prevailed as the general custom. However, one should remember that Cyprian's motivation for infant baptism differs from the motivation offered by those churches who profess infant baptism since the Reformation. At least thirteen centuries of continued development should be observed. Yet, the views of Cyprian laid the foundation.

CHAPTER 14

Eusebius of Caesarea

Eusebius Pamphili was born in about 263 probably at Caesarea in Palestine. He established his famous school at Caesarea, a centre of learning, and built up a large library. Out of respect for Pamphilus, his teacher and spiritual father, Eusebius called himself Eusebius Pamphili.

During the persecution of Caesarea, Eusebius was imprisoned. He escaped death by fleeing to Tyre and Egypt, but here too he was consigned to prison. Shortly after Constantine restored peace in 313, Eusebius was made bishop of Caesarea. Eusebius, a favourite of the Emperor Constantine, held a prominent place at the Council of Nicaea. He led the central group in order to reconcile the parties of Arius and Alexander. Even though it seems as if he was more in agreement with Arius, he eventually voted with the majority and signed the Nicene Creed. Soon afterwards Eusebius joined the adversaries of Nicaea. He took part in the synod of Tyre in 335 which fraudulently excommunicated Athanasius. Eusebius died in 339 or 340.

Eusebius was a prolific writer. His most celebrated work is his *Ecclesiastical History*. Because of this very important work, Eusebius is traditionally called the father of church history. Since Eusebius was such a prominent person in the history of the church, it was decided to include him in this study. However, his works provide us with very little information as regards the practice of baptism in the early church. For the sake of completeness we will nevertheless look at two extracts from Eusebius' writings.

The only baptismal issue which is mentioned by Eusebius, is the question of rebaptism. We have already seen in previous chapters that the church was divided on the question whether those who came from heretical groups to the orthodox church should be rebaptized or not. Eusebius also bears testimony to this issue and says as follows:

> Cornelius, having held the episcopate in the city of Rome about three years, was succeeded by Lucius. He died in less than eight months, and transmitted his office to Stephen. Dionysius wrote to him the first of his letters on baptism, as no small controversy had arisen as to whether those who had turned from any heresy should be purified by baptism. For the ancient custom prevailed in regard to such, that they should receive only the laying on of hands with prayers. First of all, Cyprian, pastor of the parish of Carthage, maintained that they should not be received except they had been purified from their error by baptism. But Stephen considering it unnecessary to add any innovation contrary to the tradition which had been held from the beginning, was very indignant at this. (*Ecclesiastical History* 7,2-3)

At another place Eusebius quotes Dionysius, the bishop of the Alexandrians, as saying:

> I received this rule and ordinance from our blessed father, Heraclas. For those who came over from heresies, although they had apostatized from the Church, – or rather had not apostatized, but seemed to meet with them, yet were charged with resorting to some false teacher, – when he had expelled them from the Church he did not receive them back, though they entreated for it, until they had publicly reported all things which they had heard

from their adversaries; but then he received them without requiring of them another baptism. For they had formerly received the Holy Spirit from him. (*Ecclesiastical History* 7,7)

Unfortunately Eusebius, the historian, does not provide us with any other information concerning the mode of baptism or the age of the baptismal candidates. Nevertheless, it seems that Eusebius suggests that a person who had been baptized as a Christian and then apostatized, was not to be rebaptized. The above passages do not seem to refer to persons who had received the baptism administered by other religions and then, on becoming Christians, were not rebaptized. These probably did receive the Christian baptism since the baptisms of other religions were not recognized.

CHAPTER 15

Cyril of Jerusalem

The place and date of birth of Cyril are unknown but it is generally thought that he was born in Jerusalem about 315. Cyril was elected bishop of Jerusalem in 348. During his life he was deeply involved in the Trinitarian controversy. Since Cyril found himself at odds with both the Arians and the 'homoousians' (a Nicene term asserting that the Son and the Father is of the same substance), he had a stormy career. Consequently he was expelled three times from his see. In 378 he regained his diocese but eight years later he died.

The most important surviving work of Cyril is his *Catechetical Lectures*. This work consists of lectures and homilies which were addressed to catechumens who were to be baptized. Cyril delivered these lectures about the year 350. They have been preserved for us because a listener took them down in shorthand, according to a scribal note in several manuscripts. This work comprises two main sections. The first section consists of a *Procatechesis*, or introductory discourse, and eighteen *Catecheses*, or pre-baptismal lectures, which give us an interesting picture of the preparation for baptism in use at the time. The second section comprising five lectures or *Mystagogical Catecheses* were addressed to newly baptized persons and deals with the sacraments which the neophytes had received, namely baptism, confirmation and the eucharist. Some scholars do challenge the Cyrilline authorship of the *Mystagogical Catecheses*, but Quasten (1975:III.366) says in his authoritative work that we do not have enough evidence to either establish or disprove Cyril's authorship. Nevertheless, it should be clear from the discussion above that the work *Catechetical Lectures* is an important witness to the ritual and doctrine of baptism in the fourth century and therefore very relevant to our study. Unfortunately, it cannot, of course, be quoted here in its entirety. It was therefore decided to quote just one of the 23 lectures in its entirety because this will give a very good idea of the trend of the work as a whole. The contents of the other lectures are more or less consistent with this lecture. In this lecture we are provided with an illuminating picture of the practice of baptism in the fourth century. There is not one sentence in the rest of the work which confutes these conclusions.

Cyril quotes Rom. 6:3 and 6:4 and then proceeds with a discussion:

> 'Do you not know that all we who have been baptized into Christ Jesus have been baptized into his death? ... since you are not under law but under grace.'
> 1. These daily introductions into the Mysteries, and new instructions, which are the announcements of new truths, are profitable to us; and most of all to you, who have been renewed from an old state to a new. Therefore, I shall necessarily lay before you the sequel of yesterday's Lecture, that you may learn of what those things, which were done by you in the inner chamber, were symbolical.
> 2. As soon, then, as you entered, you put off your tunic; and this was an image of putting off the old man with his deeds. Having stripped yourselves, you were naked; in this also imitating Christ, who was stripped naked on the Cross, and by His nakedness put off from Himself the principalities and powers, and openly triumphed over them on the tree. For since the adverse powers made their lair in your members, you may no longer wear that old garment; I do not at all mean this visible one, but the old man, which grows corrupt in the lusts of deceit. May the soul which has once put him off, never again put him

on, but say with the Spouse of Christ in the Song of Songs: 'I have put off my garment, how shall I put it on?' O wondrous thing! You were naked in the sight of all, and were not ashamed; for truly you bore the likeness of the first-formed Adam, who was naked in the garden, and was not ashamed.

3. Then, when you were stripped, you were anointed with exorcised oil, from the very hairs of your head to your feet, and were made partakers of the good olive-tree, Jesus Christ. For you were cut off from the wild olive-tree, and grafted into the good one, and were made to share the fatness of the true olive-tree. The exorcised oil therefore was a symbol of the participation of the fatness of Christ, being a charm to drive away every trace of hostile influence. For as the breathing of the saints, and the invocation of the Name of God, like fiercest flame, scorch and drive out evil spirits, so also this exorcised oil receives such virtue by the invocation of God and by prayer, as not only to burn and cleanse away the traces of sins, but also to chase away all the invisible powers of the evil one.

4. After these things, you were led to the holy pool of Divine Baptism, as Christ was carried from the Cross to the Sepulchre which is before our eyes. And each of you was asked, whether he believed in the name of the Father, and of the Son, and of the Holy Ghost, and you made that saving confession, and descended three times into the water, and ascended again; here also hinting by a symbol at the three days burial of Christ. For as our Saviour passed three days and three nights in the heart of the earth, so you also in your first ascent out of the water, represented the first day of Christ in the earth, and by your descent, the night; for as he who is in the night no longer sees, but he who is in the day, remains in the light, so in the descent, as in the night, you saw nothing, but in ascending again you were as in the day. And at the self-

same moment you were both dying and being born; and that Water of salvation was at once your grave and your mother. And what Solomon spoke of others will suit you also; for he said, in that case: 'There is a time to bear and a time to die.' But to you, in the reverse order, there was a time to die and a time to be born; and one and the same time effected both of these, and your birth went hand in hand with your death.

5. O strange and inconceivable thing! We did not really die, we were not really buried, we were not really crucified and raised again; but our imitation was in a figure, and our salvation in reality. Christ was actually crucified, and actually buried, and truly rose again; and all these things He has freely bestowed upon us, that we, sharing His sufferings by imitation, might gain salvation in reality. O surpassing loving-kindness! Christ received nails in His undefiled hands and feet, and suffered anguish; while on me, without pain or toil, by the fellowship of His suffering He freely bestows salvation.

6. Let no one then suppose that Baptism is merely the grace of remission of sins, or further, that of adoption; as John's was a baptism conferring only remission of sins: whereas we know full well, that as it purges our sins, and ministers to us the gift of the Holy Ghost, so also it is the counterpart of the sufferings of Christ. For this cause Paul just now cried aloud and said: 'Or are you ignorant that all we who were baptized into Christ Jesus, were baptized into His death? We were buried therefore with Him by baptism into His death.' These words he spoke to some who were disposed to think that Baptism ministers to us the remission of sins, and adoption, but has not further the fellowship also, by representation, of Christ's true sufferings.

7. In order therefore that we might learn, that whatsoever things Christ endured, for us and for our salvation, He suffered them in reality and not in appearance, and that

we also are made partakers of His sufferings, Paul cried with all exactness of truth. 'For if we have been planted together with the likeness of His death, we shall be also with the likeness of His resurrection.' Well has he said, 'planted together'. For since the true Vine was planted in this place we also, by partaking in the Baptism of death, have been planted together with Him. And fix your mind with much attention on the words of the Apostle. He said not 'For if we have been planted together with His death,' but, 'with the likeness of His death.' For in Christ's case there was death in reality, for His soul was really separated from His body, and real burial, for His holy body was wrapped in pure linen; and everything happened really to Him; but in your case there was only a likeness of death and sufferings, whereas of salvation there was not a likeness but a reality. (*Mystagogical Catechesis* 2)

This description of baptism resembles the contemporary accounts which we find in Etheria's *Travels* (chapter 22) and in the *Didascalia Apostolorum* (see chapter 11). It proves how the celebration and theology of adult baptism, as described above, prevailed in the churches during the fourth century.

CHAPTER 16

Asterius the Sophist

Before Asterius became a Christian he was a rhetorician and philosopher by profession, hence his name Asterius the Sophist. As such he was distinguished from Asterius of Amasea who lived towards the end of the fourth century while Asterius the Sophist died about A.D. 340. During the Christian persecution under the Emperor Maximinus, Asterius the Sophist apostatized by submitting to the Roman decree which required Christians to offer sacrifice to the Emperor. On account of his apostasy he was also known as Asterius the Sacrificer. Asterius strongly supported the Arian heresy and as such he was once more known as Asterius the Arian.

Asterius lived at a time when baptism was strongly linked to a particular interpretation of John 3:5 'unless a person is born of water and the Spirit he cannot enter the Kingdom of God.' The phrase 'born of water' was understood in reference to baptism as the unconditional prerequisite of being saved. In fact baptism was regarded as the assurance or guarantee that a person will be allowed to enter the kingdom of heaven. Without having been baptized a person was doomed. Ambrosius of Mailand, who was a contemporary of Asterius of Amasea, states explicitly in his *On Abraham* II, 11, 84 (citing John 3:5) that if a person, even an infant, might die without having been baptized, it is to be assumed that such a person will have no share in God's kingdom.

Early Christian leaders who subscribed to this point of view naturally advocated a baptism as early as possible. Asterius determined that the eighth day after birth would be the best time. His motivation for this point of view comes from his commentary on the Psalms, especially *On Psalm VI*. In the Hebrew text of Psalm 6 the note given at the beginning of the psalm reads 'for the choirmaster, for strings, for the eighth, a psalm of David'. The phrase 'for the eighth' has been interpreted by many to be a musical note, the 'octachord'. Asterius, however, supplies the word 'day' to fill out the phrase, thus reading it as 'on the eighth day'.

In the second paragraph of his commentary on Psalm 6 he asks: 'Why does the Psalm have 'on the eighth' as superscript?' He then gives the following explanation:

> The old covenant acknowledged the eighth day as the day of circumcision, the new covenant acknowledged it as the resurrection from death, the day on which death was circumcised.

His next paragraph continues to explain the link between circumcision and resurrection:

> Why was circumcision performed on the eighth day? Since an infant was dressed in swaddling-clothes for the first seven days, he received circumcision on the eighth having been loosened (from the strips of cloth) as a sign of the seal of the faith of Abraham so that we also, even if we have been dressed in the swaddling-clothes of evil for a seven day period of life, bound tight by the chains of our own sins,[1] may break these chains at the end of our life and may welcome our angelic life since we have on the eighth day been cut off (literally 'circumcised') from death by our resurrection. For 'in the resurrection people do not marry (but live like angels in heaven)'.

---

[1] Asterius is probably thinking of inherited original sin, a doctrine which was gaining more acceptance at the time.

Asterius does not quote the second part of Mt. 22:30[2], but it seems necessary to be added in order to make this quotation meaningful in the context of his argument. That is to say: on the eighth day we are baptized and thus we are resurrected so that when we die we may become angels. Baptism as such affords heavenly life; it guarantees resurrection.

Note how Asterius explains the meaning and effect of baptism as he continues:

> Therefore circumcision was also given to the descending generations, so that even the Christians afterwards may learn to seal their infants to be born to them after the swaddling-clothes of the womb, even before they are wrapped in the swaddling-clothes that can be seen.

It seems that though Asterius argues for the 'eighth day' of Psalm 6 as a yardstick, he would prefer to baptize the infants even earlier since the mother's womb may be regarded as a swaddling-cloth. This is probably to ensure that the infant may receive the ability to gain resurrection from death as soon as possible. In the following extract continuing immediately upon the section quoted above, he calls baptism the circumcision of Christ (referring to Col. 2:11–12) and then states explicitly why it is so important not to delay baptism at all. Baptism is necessary for the safety of the child. If the child dies unbaptized, there is no possibility to enter the kingdom of heaven. Asterius argues as follows:

> (Christians seal their infants) through baptism by the circumcision of Christ, concerning which Paul says: 'In whom you were also circumcised by a circumcision not made by hand, having been buried with Him (= Christ) through baptism by the circumcision of Christ.' If then, the circumcision of the Jews was given to an infant early, speedily

---

[2] Mt. 22:30 reads as follows: 'At the resurrection people will neither marry nor be given in marriage; *they will be like the angels in heaven.*'

and immediately after the swaddling-clothes, how much more should the circumcision of Christ through baptism be given even more speedily to the infant for safety sake. This must be done on the one hand in order that having put on Christ as a breastplate (the infant) may not fear the demonic enemies, and on the other hand not be handed over to capture and thus become their prisoner. Pay attention to what I say; you know the score. This must be done (namely immediate baptism) so that if the infant dies, he may not depart (from this life) unsealed.

It is noteworthy that Asterius, like Cyprian, was among the first to link baptism and circumcision. Asterius subscribed to the view that baptism should be given as soon as possible, while other writers from the same period favoured a postponement of baptism until the person can understand and respond to the rite. These were the opposing views of the fourth century. Those who favoured an early baptism often resorted, like Asterius, to circumcision as a parallel. It is also noteworthy that during the first three centuries no writer, except Cyprian, ever linked baptism with circumcision. It seems plausible that Col. 2:11-12 became relevant at the time when an early baptism was debated. Some who favoured an early baptism, but not too soon, would naturally not resort to Col. 2:11-12. The same may be expected from earlier writers for whom baptism was not a warrant to enter heaven, but symbolized dying with Christ and raising up to a new life. Within such a framework Col. 2:11-12 focused on the circumcision of the heart, that is, repentance. The analogy was, therefore, remote in that circumcision applied merely to the removal of the desires of lower nature, the 'flesh'. On the other hand, within the framework of Asterius and other writers of the fourth century, the 'sealing' power of baptism was very much in focus and can, therefore, easily be equated with Jewish circumcision as the seal of God's people.

What is important, however, is to recognize that the different views on the real meaning and significance of baptism during the fourth century was at the core of the proponents of the diverse points of view. The fourth century thus became a time of diverse practices, and in the course of the development of baptismal theory and practice, the baptism of infants gradually won the day.

Asterius is a very important writer in the history of baptism. It should, however, be noted that Asterius did not argue for the role of the covenant although he did refer once to the old covenant versus the new. For Asterius the notion of resurrection (which was also a very important feature of believer's baptism) provided the essence of the significance of baptism: it safeguards one's entry into the angelic world. Without the seal of baptism a person could not hope for eternal life, in essence, resurrection.

CHAPTER 17

Basil the Great

Basil the Great was born in 330 in a family renowned for both its Christian spirit as well as its nobility and wealth. His father, Basil, was a zealous pupil of St. Gregory the Wonderworker while his mother, Emmelia, was the daughter of a martyr. Three of the sons of Basil and Emmelia became bishops (including Basil the Great), while the eldest daughter was a model of ascetic life. Despite his Christian background Basil deferred his baptism until his adult years. This talented scholar received his higher education at Caesarea, Constantinople and Athens, where he met Gregory of Nazianzus, who became his friend for life. Basil died in 379.

Most of Basil's writings have been preserved for us. In his works entitled *On Baptism* and *Exhortation to the Holy Baptism* Basil does, of course, deal with baptism. Yet, Basil's exposition is more concerned with the holy life expected from either a candidate or a person having received baptism, than with the significance and the day of baptism as such. Therefore, very little is relevant for this study since these writings have no bearing on either the age of the baptismal candidate or the rite itself. He does make a few interesting remarks in another important work of his, entitled *On the Holy Spirit*, in which he makes it clear, inter alia, that a person who has not been baptized will not be saved. Neither did he believe in the validity of heretical baptism:

> Whence is it that we are Christians? Through our faith, would be the universal answer. And in what way are we saved? Plainly because we were regenerated through the grace given in our baptism ... Whether a man has departed this life without baptism, or has received a baptism lacking in some of the requirements of the tradition, his loss is equal ... For if to me my baptism was the beginning of life, and that day of regeneration the first of days, it is plain that the utterance uttered in the grace of adoption was the most honourable of all. (*On the Spirit* 26)

To Basil faith and baptism are inseparable:

> Faith and baptism are two kindred and inseparable ways of salvation: faith is perfected through baptism, baptism is established through faith, and both are completed by the same names. For as we believe in the Father and the Son and the Holy Ghost, so are we also baptized in the name of the Father and of the Son and of the Holy Ghost: first comes the confession, introducing us to salvation, and baptism follows, setting the seal upon our assent. (*On the Spirit* 28)

Furthermore, Basil believes that there should be a distinct difference between one's life before and after baptism. He also describes the immersion of baptism as the burial of the old life:

> So Paul, the imitator of Christ, says, 'being made conformable unto his death; if by any means I might attain unto the resurrection of the dead.' How then are we made in the likeness of His death? In that we were buried with Him by baptism. What then is the manner of the burial? And what is the advantage resulting from the imitation? First of all, it is necessary that the continuity of the old life be cut. And this is impossible unless a man be born

again, according to the Lord's word; for the regeneration, as indeed the name shows, is a beginning of a second life. So before beginning the second, it is necessary to put an end to the first. For just as in the case of runners who turn and take the second course, a kind of halt and pause intervenes between the movements in the opposite direction, so also in making a change in lives it seemed necessary for death to come as mediator between the two, ending all that goes before, and beginning all that comes after. How then do we achieve the descent into hell? By imitating, through baptism, the burial of Christ. For the bodies of the baptized are, as it were, buried in the water. Baptism then symbolically signifies the putting off of the works of the flesh; as the apostle says, you were 'circumcised with the circumcision made without hands, in putting off the body of the sins of the flesh by the circumcision of Christ; buried with him in baptism.' (*On the Spirit* 35)

Basil describes a baptism which was administered by three immersions:

This then is what it is to be born again of water and of the Spirit, the being made dead being effected in the water, while our life is wrought in us through the Spirit. In three immersions, then, and with three invocations, the great mystery of baptism is performed, to the end that the type of death may be fully figured, and that by the tradition of the divine knowledge the baptized may have their souls enlightened. It follows that if there is any grace in the water, it is not of the nature of the water, but of the presence of the Spirit. (*On the Spirit* 35)

Basil's exposition of the significance and practice of baptism reflects the same features that are to be found in all the early Church Fathers' descriptions of believer's baptism.

CHAPTER 18

Gregory of Nazianzus

Gregory of Nazianzus, one of the three great Cappadocian Fathers, was born in 330. His father was a bishop and his saintly mother, the daughter of Christian parents, consecrated Gregory to God even before his birth. It is interesting to note that, despite his Christian upbringing, Gregory was baptized when he was about 28 years old. In 362 Gregory was ordained priest somewhat against his will. In 372 he was consecrated as bishop, once more against his will. Gregory died in 389. Gregory was not a prolific author, but his literary bequest consists of orations, poems and letters.

Gregory was one of the theologians who played an important part in the transition from adult baptism to infant baptism. He himself defended the baptism of children, but disapproved of infant baptism on the grounds that an infant cannot give account of his faith. However, Gregory also spoke out against the practice which prevailed during his time, namely of delaying baptism until one's deathbed. He said it was too risky since calamity might strike one unexpectedly and then that person dies without having been washed from his sins. He therefore argued that one should baptize a person as soon as possible, but not before three years of age because someone younger than this age would not be able to understand the sacrament. Later on other theologians built on Gregory's arguments in their defence of infant baptism. It is noteworthy that until this time the covenant idea was never proposed in the theological debate on baptism.

In order to gain insight into Gregory's beliefs concerning baptism, we will quote extensively from a sermon which he delivered on January 6, 381 and which deals with this theme. This oration provides an important insight into the theology of baptism which prevailed during the second half of the fourth century.

In the first place, Gregory also believed in the cleansing function of baptism:

> Such is the grace and power of baptism; not an overwhelming of the world as of old, but a purification of the sins of each individual, and a complete cleansing from all the bruises and stains of sin. (Chapter 7)

We have already seen that by the fourth century many Christians preferred to delay/postpone their baptism until their deathbed in order to wash away more sins. Gregory spoke out against this practice and he advised his followers not to defer their baptism:

> Let us then be baptized that we may win the victory; let us partake of the cleansing waters, more purifying than hyssop, purer than the legal blood, more sacred than the ashes of the heifer sprinkling the unclean, and providing a temporary cleansing of the body, but not a complete taking away of sin; for if once purged, why should they need further purification? Let us be baptized today, that we suffer not violence tomorrow; and let us not put off the blessing as if it were an injury, nor wait till we get more wicked that more may be forgiven us. (Chapter 11)

Gregory argued that it was better not to wait until disaster strikes before one asks to be baptized:

Why wait for a fever to bring you this blessing, and refuse it from God? Why will you have it through lapse of time, and not through reason? Why will you owe it to a plotting friend, and not to a saving desire? Why will you receive it of force and not of free will; of necessity rather than of liberty? Why must you hear of your death from another, rather than think of it as even now present? Why do you seek for drugs which will do no good, or the sweat of the crisis, when the sweat of death is perhaps upon you? Heal yourself before your extremity; have pity upon yourself the only true healer of your disease; apply to yourself the really saving medicine; while you are still sailing with a favourite breeze fear shipwreck, and you will be in less danger of it, if you make use of your terror as a helper. (Chapter 12)

Gregory said that it was dangerous to defer one's baptism. One might meet death unexpectedly and that would mean that one would die without having been baptized:

'Give to me,' he (= the Evil One) says, 'the present, and to God the future; to me your youth, and to God old age; to me your pleasures, and to Him your uselessness.' How great is the danger that surrounds you. How many the unexpected mischances. War has expended you; or an earthquake overwhelmed you; or the sea swallowed you up; or a wild beast carried you off; or a sickness killed you; or a crumb going the wrong way (a most insignificant thing, but what is easier than for a man to die, though you are so proud of the divine image); or a too freely indulged drinking bout; or a wind knocked you down; or a horse ran away with you; or a drug maliciously scheming against you, or perhaps found to be deleterious when meant to be wholesome; or an inhuman judge; or an inexorable executioner; or any of the things which make the change swiftest and beyond the power of human aid. (Chapter 14)

Gregory then elaborates on the advantages of being baptized:

> For we do not command, we exhort; and we would receive something of you for your own profit, and the common security of you both. And in one word, there is no state of life and no occupation to which Baptism is not profitable. You who are a free man, be curbed by it; you who are in slavery, be made of equal rank; you who are in grief, receive comfort; let the gladsome be disciplined; the poor receive riches that cannot be taken away; the rich be made capable of being good stewards of their possessions. (Chapter 18)

Many Christians, however, preferred to rather delay baptism so that they could still enjoy the pleasures of this world. They believed that they could obtain this grace towards the end of their lives and by doing so all the sins committed during their lives would be washed away. They even referred to the parable of the vineyard to defend their point of view:

> But some will say: 'What shall I gain, if, when I am preoccupied by baptism, and have cut off myself by my haste from the pleasures of life, when it was in my power to give the reins to pleasure, and then to obtain grace? For the labourers in the vineyard who had worked the longest time gained nothing thereby, for equal wages were given to the very last.' You have delivered me from some trouble, whoever you are who say this, because you have at last with much difficulty told the secret of your delay; and though I cannot applaud your shiftiness, I do applaud your confession. But come hither and listen to the interpretation of the parable, that you may not be injured by Scripture for want of information. First of all, there is no

question here of baptism, but of those who believe at different times and enter the good vineyard of the Church. For from the day and hour at which each believed, from that day and hour he is required to work. (Chapter 20)

Gregory then points out that this interpretation of the parable is wrong and also very risky:

And next, the workmen who receive the wages are those who have entered, not those who have missed, the vineyard; which last is like to be your case ... But since there is a risk of your being altogether shut out of the vineyard through your bargaining, and losing the capital through stopping to pick up little gains, do let yourselves be persuaded by my words to forsake the false interpretations and contradictions, and to come forward without arguing to receive the Gift, lest you should be snatched away before you realize your hopes, and should find out that it was to your own loss that you devised these sophistries. (Chapter 21)

It is clear from what Gregory writes that very many people of his day deferred baptism because of various reasons:

Others know and honour the Gift, but put it off; some through laziness, some through greediness. Others are not in a position to receive it, perhaps on account of infancy, or some perfectly involuntary circumstance through which they are prevented from receiving it, even if they wish. (Chapter 22)

In Gregory's time the confession of sins and exorcism were still integral parts of the rite of baptism:

Do not disdain to confess your sins, knowing how John baptized, that by present shame you may escape from future shame (for this too is a part of the future punishment); and prove that you really hate sin by making a show of it openly, and triumphing over it as worthy of contempt. Do not reject the medicine of exorcism, nor refuse it because of its length. This too is a touchstone of your right disposition for grace. What labour have you to do compared with that of the Queen of Ethiopia, who arose and came from the utmost part of the earth to see the wisdom of Solomon? (Chapter 27)

Gregory played an important part in swinging public opinion from one extreme (baptism at deathbed) to the other extreme (baptism of children):

Have you an infant child? Do not let sin get any opportunity, but let him be sanctified from his childhood; from his very tenderest age let him be consecrated by the Spirit. Do you fear the Seal on account of the weakness of nature? O what a small-souled mother, and of how little faith! Why, Hannah even before Samuel was born promised him to God, and after his birth consecrated him at once, and brought him up in the priestly habit, not fearing anything in human nature, but trusting in God. You have no need of amulets or incantations, with which the Devil also comes in, stealing worship from God for himself in the minds of vainer men. Give your child the Trinity, that great and noble Guard. (Chapter 17)

However, it is very important to note that Gregory nevertheless did not approve of the baptism of infants because they could not profess their faith. He therefore believed that baptism should not be administered to children less than three years of age:

> Be it so, some will say, in the case of those who ask for baptism; what have you to say about those who are still small children, and conscious neither of the loss nor of the grace? Are we to baptize them too? Certainly, if any danger presses. For it is better that they should be unconsciously sanctified than that they should depart unsealed and uninitiated. A proof of this is found in the circumcision on the eighth day, which was a sort of typical seal, and was conferred on children before they had the use of reason. And so is the anointing of the doorposts, which preserved the firstborn, though applied to things which had no consciousness. But in respect of others I give my advice to wait till the end of the third year, or a little more or less, when they may be able to listen and to answer something about the sacrament; that, even though they do not perfectly understand it, yet at any rate they may know the outlines; and then to sanctify them in soul and body with the great sacrament of our consecration. For this is how the matter stands; at that time they begin to be responsible for their lives, when reason is matured, and they learn the mystery of life (for of sins of ignorance owing to their tender years they have no account to give), and it is far more profitable on all accounts to be fortified by the Font, because of the sudden assault of danger that befalls us, stronger than our helpers. (Chapter 28)

It is important to note that Gregory is not saying that circumcision was replaced by baptism. Note also that he employs a second parallel, namely, the anointing of the doorposts prior to the exodus from Egypt. He is merely pointing to *one* similarity (namely very early childhood) between circumcision and the anointing of the doorposts on the one hand, and baptism on the other. Moreover, the idea of the covenant played no role whatsoever in the theology of the early church leading up to the institution of infant baptism. As a matter of fact, the washing away of sins as a *sine qua non* to enter the kingdom of heaven was the main theological argument for conferring baptism as early as possible. The practice of confessing one's belief was, nevertheless, still upheld as a general practice since Gregory maintains that baptism before the age of three years is not advisable. The allowance for an earlier age was condoned merely in pressing situations where an early death was imminent. However, this allowance along with a psychological 'play-it-safe' may have been an important injunction for parents not to defer the baptism of their children for too long. Baptism as a sacrament, i.e. as a performative rite which accomplishes something substantial (and not as a symbol signifying dying with Christ and being raised to a new life as in the earlier stages of Christian baptism), gradually became the dominant theology underlying the rite of baptism as a washing away of sins. Gregory's point of view is an important possible step towards a more general baptism of infants which seems to have gained momentum since the latter part of the fourth century. Yet one should be cautious not to jump to the conclusion that Gregory's viewpoint represents a widespread opinion. Many other writers during the fourth century still maintained the requirement of confession of sin as a preliminary to baptism without making any allowance for infants. Gregory's views should rather be seen as a particular point in a larger process that contained the seeds for later developments.

CHAPTER 19

Gregory of Nyssa

Gregory of Nyssa, one of the three great Cappadocians, was the brother of Basil and was born in 335. He received his education chiefly from his brother Basil. Gregory was consecrated bishop of Nyssa in 371 against his will. In 376 he was deposed by a Synod of Arian bishops, but in 378 he was restored to his see. He died in 394.

The works of Gregory of Nyssa shed very little light on the rite of baptism as such. However, since Gregory, as one of the Cappadocian Fathers, was a prominent figure in the early church, it was nevertheless decided to include him in this study. About 385 Gregory of Nyssa composed his *Catechesis.* In this writing there is a section which deals with baptism. Let us now look at a few quotations from this section.

In the first place Gregory talks about the mystical character of baptism and says:

> But the descent into the water, and the threefold immersion of the person in it, involves another mystery. (*Catechesis* 35)

Note the phrase 'descent into the water' as well as the threefold character of the administration of baptism.

Gregory also believed in the cleansing efficacy of baptism:

Since, then, there is a cleansing virtue in fire and water, they who by the mystic water have washed away the defilement of their sin have no further need of the other form of purification, while they who have not been admitted to that form of purgation have to be purified by fire. (*Catechesis* 35)

According to Gregory baptism was necessary for salvation:

For common sense as well as the teaching of Scripture show that it is impossible for one who has not thoroughly cleansed himself from all the stains arising from evil to be admitted amongst the heavenly company. This is a thing which, though little in itself, is the beginning and foundation of great blessings ...
Now, the work properly belonging to the Divine energy is the salvation of those who need it; and this salvation proves effectual by means of the cleansing in the water; and he that has been so cleansed will participate in Purity; and true Purity is Deity. You see, then, how small a thing it is in its beginning, and how easily effected; I mean, faith and water, the first residing within the will, the latter being the nursery companion of the life of man. But as to the blessing which springs from these two things, oh! how great and how wonderful it is, that it should imply relationship with Deity itself! (*Catechesis* 36)

Thus it is clear that Gregory's theology on baptism was in line with the theology of his time.

CHAPTER 20

Ambrose

Ambrose was born in 339 at Trier. He studied rhetoric in preparation for a public career. Toward 370 Ambrose attained the office of consul. In 373 he was elected as bishop of Milan while he was still a catechumen. However, he was baptized on November 24 and a week later, on December 1, his consecration was performed. Thereafter Ambrose donated all his possessions to the church for charitable purposes. In 397 he fell ill and died on April 4, 397.

Ambrose wrote a book entitled *The Sacraments*. It was composed before A.D. 392 and it consists of six short addresses which were delivered to the newly baptized. These addresses were delivered on six successive days, beginning on the Tuesday of Easter week and continuing till the following Sunday. This work provides us with an extensive description of baptism as practised in the fourth century.

Ambrose tells us that the act of baptism was preceded by the anointment of the baptismal candidate:

> (4) We have come to the font; you have entered. Consider whom you have seen, what you have answered; consider; repeat everything carefully. A Levite meets you; an elder meets you; you are anointed as an athlete of Christ, as if you are to contend in the contest of this world. You have professed the struggles of your contest ... (*Sacraments* 1.4)

Thereafter the candidate had to renounce the devil and the pleasures of this world:

> (5) When he asked you: 'Do you renounce the devil and his works?' – what did you answer? 'I do renounce.' 'Do you renounce the world and its pleasures?' What did you answer? 'I do renounce.' (*Sacraments* 1.5)

Ambrose says that when the candidate approaches the font and notices the ordinary elements, he often doubts the cleansing character of baptism. However, he should remember that it is only during baptism that the true meaning of this water becomes clear:

> (9) Then you drew nearer; you saw the font; you also saw the priest above the font. I cannot doubt that that could not have fallen upon your mind, which fell upon that Syrian Naaman, for, though he was cleansed, yet he doubted first. (15) What, then, is the meaning of this? You have seen water: not all water cures, but the water which has the grace of Christ does cure ... Water does not cure unless the Ghost descends and consecrates that water, as you have read that, when our Lord Jesus Christ gave the form of baptism, He came to John, and John said to Him: 'I ought to be baptized by you; and you come to me?' Christ answered: 'Let it be so now: for so it becomes us to fulfil all justice.' Note that all justice is constituted in baptism. (16) Therefore, why did Christ descend, except that that flesh of yours might be cleansed, the flesh which He took over from our condition? For no washing away of His sins was necessary for Christ, 'who did no sin', but it was necessary for us who remain subject to sin. (*Sacraments* 1.9 & 15-16)

Thereafter the catechumen was asked three times to confess his faith in the Trinity and after each confession he was immersed:

> (20) You were asked: 'Do you believe in God the Father Almighty?' You answered: 'I do believe', and you dipped, that means: you were buried. Again you were asked: 'Do you believe in our Lord Jesus Christ and in His cross?' You answered: 'I do believe', and you dipped. So you were also buried together with Christ. A third time you were asked: 'Do you believe also in the Holy Ghost?' You answered: 'I do believe', you dipped a third time. (*Sacraments* 2.20)

After the immersion of the believer an announcement by the priest (i.e. bishop) followed:

> (24) So you dipped; you went to the priest. What did he say to you? He said: 'God the Almighty Father, who regenerated you by water and the Holy Ghost and forgave you your sins, He will anoint you unto everlasting life.' See, unto what you were anointed. He said: 'Unto everlasting life.' Do not prefer this life to that life. (*Sacraments* 2.24)

Thereafter follows a ceremony of the washing of the feet. It is most interesting to note that Ambrose explicitly says that in Rome the baptismal rite does not include the washing of the feet. The rite as such, therefore, seems to have been the same in Rome as described by Ambrose. He also says that other churches usually follow the Church in Rome in all things. This may suggest that the rest of the baptismal rite, as we have it in this work, was fairly generally accepted by churches in the fourth century, while the ceremony of the washing of the feet may have been more sporadic in occurrence. Ambrose comments on this situation as follows:

(4) You came up from the font. What followed? You heard the reading. The highest priest girded ... washed your feet. What mystery is this? You have heard that the Lord had washed the feet of the other disciples and thereafter He went to Peter. Peter said to Him: 'Do you wash my feet?' That is: 'Do you, Lord, wash the feet of a servant; do you without stain wash my feet; do you, the creator of the heavens, wash my feet?' You can read this also elsewhere: He went to John and John said to Him: 'I need to be baptized by you, and you come to me? I am a sinner, and have you come to a sinner, that you who have not sinned may put aside your sins?' Behold all justice, behold humility, behold grace, behold sanctification. He said: 'If I wash not your feet, you shall have no part with me.' (5) We are not ignorant of the fact that the Church in Rome does not have this custom, whose practice and form we follow in all things. Yet it does not have the custom of washing the feet. So note: perhaps on account of the many people involved this practice declined. (*Sacraments* 3.4-5)

After these ceremonies the baptismal candidate was considered to be purified from his sins:

(5) There follows your coming to the altar. You came; the angels watched; they saw you coming, and that human condition which before was stained with the shadowy squalor of sins they saw suddenly shining bright, and then they said: 'Who is this person who is coming up from the desert whitewashed?' So the angels also marvelled. Do you wish to know how they marvelled? Hear the Apostle Peter saying that those things have been conferred on you which the angels also wanted to see. Hear again. It says: 'The eye has not seen, nor the ear heard what things God has prepared for them who love Him.' (*Sacraments* 4.5)

As in many other descriptions of the ceremony of baptism (see for example Justin in chapter 4 of this book), the catechumens partook of the eucharist after they were baptized:

> (8) You have come to the altar; you have seen the sacraments placed on the altar; and indeed you have marvelled at what is taking place. Yet what is taking place is customary and known ... (21) The priest speaks. He says: '... On the day before He suffered He took bread in His holy hands, looked toward heaven, toward you, holy Father, Almighty, eternal God, giving thanks, blessed, broke and having broken it, gave it to His Apostles and His disciples, saying: 'Take and eat of this, all of you; for this is my body, which shall be broken for many". (*Sacraments* 4.8-21)

Ambrose, however, also wrote a treatise entitled *The Mysteries*. This tract, too, consists of addresses given to the newly baptized during Easter Week and deals with the rites and meaning of the sacraments, including baptism. Ambrose's *Mysteries* is very similar in content to his *Sacraments*. Let us, nevertheless, look at *The Mysteries*, which will confirm our findings concerning baptism, which were derived from *The Sacraments*.

In the first place Ambrose tells us that questions were put to the baptismal candidate who after having responded, had to renounce the devil and the present world:

> (5) After this the Holy of holies was opened to you, you entered the sanctuary of regeneration. Remember what you were asked, and remember what you responded! You renounced the Devil and his works, the world with its luxury and pleasures. Your words are kept not in the tomb of the dead, but in the book of the living ... (7) You entered, therefore, that you might recognize your adver-

sary, whom you were to renounce to his face, then you turned to the east. For he who renounces the devil, turns toward Christ, recognizes Him by a direct glance. (*Mysteries* 5-7)

The act of questioning and consecration was done by the bishop:

(8) What did you see? Water, certainly, but not water alone; you saw deacons ministering there, and the bishop questioning and consecrating... (*Mysteries* 8)

It was clear from *The Sacraments* that the questions put to the candidate were meant to lead to a profession of faith. This becomes again evident when one reads how these candidates responded.

(28) You went down, then (into the water), remember what you replied to the questions, that you believe in the Father, that you believe in the Son, that you believe in the Holy Spirit. The statement there is not: I believe in a greater and in a lesser and in a lowest person, but you are bound by the same guarantee of your own voice, to believe in the Son in like manner as you believe in the Father; and to believe in the Holy Spirit in like manner as you believe in the Son, with this one exception, that you confess that you must believe in the cross of the Lord Jesus alone. (*Mysteries* 28)

In *The Sacraments* we read about an unction which preceded the act of baptism. In *The Mysteries* we read of another unction which followed the baptismal ceremony:

(29) After this, you went up to the priest. Consider what followed. Was it not that of which David speaks: 'Like the ointment upon the head, which went down to the beard,

even Aaron's beard'? This is the ointment of which Solomon, too, says: 'Your Name is ointment poured out, therefore have the maidens loved You and drawn You.' How many souls regenerated this day have loved You, Lord Jesus, and have said: 'Draw us after You; we are running after the odour of Your garments,' that they might drink in the odour of Your resurrection. (*Mysteries* 29)

We again read about the ceremony of the washing of the feet:

(31) You went up from the font; remember the Gospel lesson. For our Lord Jesus Christ in the Gospel washed the feet of His disciples. When He came to Simon Peter, Peter said: 'You will never wash my feet.' He did not perceive the mystery, and therefore he refused the service, for he thought that the humility of the servant would be injured, if he patiently allowed the Lord to minister to him. And the Lord answered him: 'If I wash not your feet, you will have no part with Me.' Peter, hearing this, replies: 'Lord not my feet only, but also my hands and my head.' The Lord answered: 'He who is washed needs only to wash his feet but is wholly clean.'
(32) Peter was clean, but he must wash his feet, for he had sin by succession from the first man, when the serpent overthrew him and persuaded him to sin. His feet were therefore washed, that hereditary sins might be done away, for our own sins are remitted through baptism. (*Mysteries* 31-2)

As in other accounts of the rite of baptism, we notice that the catechumens were given white garments to wear after they were baptized:

(34) After this white robes were given to you as a sign that you were putting off the covering of sins, and putting on the chaste veil of innocence, of which the prophet said: 'You shall sprinkle me with hyssop and I shall be cleansed, You shall wash me and I shall be made whiter than snow.' For he who is baptized is seen to be purified both according to the Law and according to the Gospel: according to the Law, because Moses sprinkled the blood of the lamb with a bunch of hyssop; according to the Gospel, because Christ's garments were white as snow, when in the Gospel He showed forth the glory of His Resurrection. He, then, whose guilt is remitted is made whiter than snow. So that God said by Isaiah: 'though your sins be as scarlet, I will make them white as snow.' (*Mysteries* 34)

Once again we read that baptism was followed by a participation of the eucharist:

(43) The cleansed person, rich in these adornments, hastens to the altar of Christ, saying: 'I will go to the altar of God, to God who makes glad my youth'; for having laid aside the slough of ancient error, renewed with an eagle's youth, he hastens to approach that heavenly feast. He comes, and seeing the holy altar arranged, cries out: 'You have prepared a table in my sight.' David introduces the man as speaking, where he says: 'The Lord feeds me, and nothing shall be wanting to me, in a place of good pasture has He placed me. He has led me forth by the water of refreshment.' And later: 'For though I walk in the midst of the shadow of death, I will fear no evils, for You are with me. Your rod and Your staff have comforted me. You have prepared in my sight a table against them that trouble me. You have anointed my head with oil, and Your inebriating cup, how excellent it is!' (*Mysteries* 43)

When we come to the meaning of baptism, we see that Ambrose regarded baptism as a seal:

> (42) And then remember that you received the seal of the Spirit; the spirit of wisdom and understanding, the spirit of counsel and strength, the spirit of knowledge and godliness, and the spirit of holy fear, and preserve what you received. God the Father sealed you. Christ the Lord strengthened you, and gave the earnest of the Spirit in your heart, and you have learned in the lesson of the Apostle. (*Mysteries* 42)

Furthermore, for Ambrose the meaning of baptism was the washing away of sins. In keeping with many other Church Fathers, he interprets the narrative of Noah in the ark as a typological prefiguration of baptism. Note that Ambrose speaks of baptism as the immersion in water which washes away the sins of man:

> (10) Take another testimony. All flesh was corrupt by its iniquities. 'My Spirit,' says God, 'shall not remain among men, because they are flesh.' Whereby God shows that the grace of the Spirit is turned away by carnal impurity and the pollution of grave sin. Upon which, God, willing to restore what was lacking, sent the flood and bade just Noah go up into the ark. And he, after having, as the flood was passing off, sent forth first a raven which did not return, sent forth a dove which is said to have returned with an olive twig. You see the water, you see the wood (of the ark), you see the dove, and do you hesitate as to the mystery?
> (11) The water, then, is that in which the flesh is dipped, that all carnal sin may be washed away. All wickedness is there buried. The wood is that on which the Lord Jesus was fastened when He suffered for us. The dove is that in whose form the Holy Ghost descended, and you have

read in the New Testament, who inspires in you peace of
soul and tranquillity of mind. The raven is the figure of
sin, which goes forth and does not return, if, in you, too,
inwardly and outwardly righteousness be preserved.
(*Mysteries* 10-11)

Ambrose teaches the catechumens that baptism is much more than that which is seen by the naked eye. Not every descent into the water purifies a man from his sins, but only when it happens during the rite of baptism:

(19) The reason why you were told before not to believe only what you saw was that you might not say perchance, 'This is that great mystery 'which eye has not seen, nor ear heard, neither has it entered into the heart of man'. I see water, which I have been used to see every day. Is that water to cleanse me now, that water in which I have so often bathed without ever being cleansed?' By this you may recognize that water does no cleanse without the Spirit. (*Mysteries* 19)

Ambrose also regards baptism as a regeneration. As a matter of fact he believes that one cannot be saved, unless one is baptized:

(20) Therefore read that the three witnesses in baptism, the water, the blood, and the Spirit, are one, for if you take away one of these, the sacrament of baptism does not exist. For what is water without the cross of Christ? A common element, without any sacramental effect. Nor, again, is there the sacrament of regeneration without water: 'For except a man be born again of water and of the Spirit, he cannot enter into the kingdom of God.' Now, even the catechumen believes in the cross of the Lord Jesus, wherewith he too is signed; but unless he is baptized in the Name of the Father, and of the Son, and

of the Holy Spirit, he cannot receive remission of sins nor gain the gift of spiritual grace. (*Mysteries* 20)

Ambrose is one of the authors who has left us with an explicit description of the complete rite of baptism prevalent in his day. It is noteworthy that several fourth century authors provide us with such detailed descriptions as will also be seen in following chapters. Fourth century authors are valuable sources since they were generally more explicit in describing various aspects of early Christian theology and ceremonies.

CHAPTER 21

Apostolic Constitutions (Constitutiones Apostolorum)

The termination of the first three centuries A.D. occasioned a new era in which early Christianity was no longer in conflict with the State. This new time of relief is especially evident in the development of the liturgy as Christian communities began to increase rapidly. The fourth century saw the first sacramentaries to emerge as full-fledged formulations of creed and practice. Eucharist, prayer and baptism began to assume a more conventionalized form and procedure. The practice of baptism as described in chapters 15, 20 and 22 may be seen as clear examples of such ceremonial developments.

During these times several liturgies developed of which the so-called *Apostolic Constitutions* affords us valuable information concerning the rite of baptism. It is especially important in that it formalized the theological trends of the day, which emphasized the fact that baptism guarantees one's entrance into the Kingdom of heaven. The delay of baptism was increasingly seen as a risk. While believer's baptism was still widely practised, as was shown in the previous chapters (as well as in chapter 22), children, and eventually infants, were also baptized as a safeguard.

The sixth book of the *Apostolic Constitutions* is quite explicit:

> But also the one who by reason of contempt is unwilling to be baptized, will be condemned as an unbeliever and

will be reproached as ungrateful and foolish. For the Lord says: 'Unless one is baptized by water and Spirit, one cannot enter the Kingdom of Heaven.' And again: 'He who believes and is baptized will be saved, but he who believes not will be condemned.' The person who says 'when I am about to die I will be baptized so that I may not sin any more and (thus) defile my baptism,' is so ignorant of God and his own nature that he is forgetful of what the Lord says: 'Do not delay to turn unto the Lord, for you do not know what tomorrow will bring.' Baptize also your young children and bring them up in the teaching and admonishing of God. For He says: 'Let the children come unto me and forbid them not.'(chapter 15, 5-7)

The children referred to are designated by the Greek word, νήπιος. This term usually pertains to very young children. Though it is not absolutely certain how old these children were, one could perhaps follow Gregory of Nazianzus in assuming that young children (not infants) would be implied, since these were also required to partake in the ritual of responding to the questions put by the priest or bishop. Nevertheless, the prescriptions advocated by Asterius the Sophist (see chapter 16) who required baptism to be administered on the eighth day after birth, may suggest that in the prescriptions of the *Apostolic Constitutions* even infants were involved. It is, however, difficult to determine precisely how far Asterius was followed in his theology. In fact, Asterius used the word βρεφος, baby, in his writings. It could well be said that Asterius took the matter further than the *Apostolic Constitutions* and many other early Church Fathers, in linking baptism to circumcision, and therefore he obviously advocated an earlier age.

Perhaps the best way of judging the matter may be to conclude that although children were baptized occasionally, the fourth century reduced the age to very young children, and in the writings of Asterius these are definitely babies. The *Apostolic*

Constitutions may, therefore, not reflect a fully developed view of the matter unless it is argued that its terminology was not carefully chosen.

CHAPTER 22

Etheria (or Egeria)

Etheria (or Egeria) was a lady pilgrim to the Holy Land in the fourth century. In the late nineteenth century a manuscript was found which proved to be the middle part of her book, *Travels*, which was lost for many centuries. In this itinerary Etheria records all the places and scenes she visited on her journey to the East which she probably undertook between 381 and 384. This cultivated lady also gives us invaluable descriptions of liturgies as celebrated in the churches which she visited. Thus this unique document casts some interesting light on the practice of baptism in the late fourth century.

She writes, inter alia, as follows:

> The following day is the Saturday, and they have normal services at nine o'clock and midday. But at three o'clock they stop keeping Saturday because they are preparing for the paschal vigil in the Great Church, namely the Martyrium. They keep their paschal vigil like us, but this one thing they add. As soon as the infants have been baptized and clothed, and left the font, they are led with the bishop straight to the Anastasis. The bishop goes into the screen of the Anastasis and after one hymn says a prayer for them. Then he returns with them to the Great Church, where all the people are keeping the vigil in their customary way. ... On each of the eight days of Easter the bishop, with all the clergy, and all the infants, that is the infants who have been baptized, all the poor ones, both

men and women, and any of the people who wish, go up to the Eleona. Then they sing hymns and have prayers in the church. (38.1-39.3)

It is important to note that the term 'infants' (Latin: *infantes*) is used figuratively for new-born babies in Christ, i.e. neophytes. This was explicitly said by the Fathers. Caesarius of Arles, for example, said in the fifth century that 'they are called infants because, although they had been born earlier in the world, they were just reborn in Christ.' (*Sermon* 205.) Furthermore, in the next excerpt Etheria explicitly describes these 'infants' as 'men and women'. It is also clear from the following passage that the questions which these 'infants' are asked, are designed for adults. Thus this section from Etheria's *Travels* provides us with invaluable evidence for the practice of adult baptism in the fourth century:

I have to add something about the way they instruct those who are to be baptized at Easter. The names are given in before the first day of Lent, which means that a presbyter takes down all the names before the beginning of the eight weeks for which Lent lasts here, as I have told you. Once the priest has all the names, on the second day of Lent at the beginning of the eight weeks, the bishop's chair is placed in the middle of the Great Church, the Martyrium, while the presbyters sit in chairs on either side of him and all the clergy stand. Then those seeking baptism are brought up one by one, men coming with their fathers and women with their mothers. As they come in one by one, the bishop asks those with them questions about them. 'Is this person leading a good life? Does he respect his parents? Is he a drunkard or a boaster?' He asks questions about all the serious vices people commit. And if his inquiries show him that someone has not committed any of these misdeeds, he himself puts down his name; but if some is accused by someone else, he commands him to go away saying: 'Amend your ways and when you have amended them, then come to the font.' He asks the men and the women the same questions. But it is not too easy for a visitor to come to baptism if he has not a witness who knows him well. Ladies and sisters, I now have to write the following so that you will not think that all this is done without explanation. They have here this custom that those who are preparing for baptism during the season of the Lenten fast, go to be exorcized by the clergy first thing in the morning, directly after the morning dismissal in the Anastasis. Soon afterwards the bishop's chair is placed in the Great Church, the Martyrium, and all those to be baptized, the men and the women, sit round the bishop in a circle. There is a place where the fathers and mothers stand, and all those of the people who are believers and who want to listen can come in and sit down. The catechumens, however, do not come in while the bishop is teaching, while the bishop teaches them about the law as follows, namely beginning from Genesis he goes through the whole Bible during the forty days. He first relates the literal meaning of each passage, then interprets its spiritual meaning. He also teaches them at this time all about the resurrection and the faith. This is called catechesis. After five weeks' teaching they receive the Creed, whose content he explains article by article in the same way as he explained the Scriptures, first literally and then spiritually. Thus all the people in these places are able to follow the Scriptures when they are read in church, since there has been teaching on all the Scriptures from six to nine in the morning all through Lent, three hours of catechesis a day. God is my witness ladies and sisters, that at ordinary services, when the bishop sits and preaches, ladies and sisters, the faithful utter exclamations, but when they come and hear him explaining the catechesis, their exclamations are far louder and louder and when it is related and interpreted like this, they ask questions on each point.

At nine o'clock they are dismissed from Catechesis, and the bishop is taken to the Anastasis while the people sing. So the dismissal is at nine, which makes three hours' teaching a day for seven weeks. But in the eighth, known as the Great Week, there is no time for them to teach if they have to carry out everything I have described above. So when seven weeks have passed, and only the week of Easter remains, the one which people here call the Great Week, the bishop comes early into the Great Church, the Martyrium. His chair is placed at the back of the apse, behind the altar, and one by one the candidates go up to the bishop, men with their fathers and women with their mothers, they recite the Creed to the bishop. When they have done so, the bishop speaks to them all and says: 'During these seven weeks you have been instructed in the whole Law of the Scriptures. You have heard not only about the faith, but also about the resurrection of the body. As catechumens, you were also able to listen to the complete content of the Creed. But the teaching about baptism itself is a much deeper mystery, and you cannot hear it while you remain catechumens. Do not think it will never be explained; you will hear it all in the Anastasis during the eight days after your dismissal from the church when you will have been baptized in the name of God. But so long as you are catechumens you cannot be told God's deep mysteries.'

Then Easter comes, and during the eight days from Easter Day to the eighth day, after the dismissal has taken place from the church, they have come with singing into the Anastasis. Soon the prayer is said and the faithful are blessed. Then the bishop stands leaning against the inner screen in the cave of the Anastasis, and interprets all that takes place at Baptism. At that time no one of the catechumens comes into the Anastasis, but all the newly baptized and any of the faithful who wish to hear the Mysteries enter into the Anastasis. The doors are kept shut so that no catechumen may enter. The bishop relates what has been done, and interprets it, and, as he does so, the applause is so loud that it can be heard far outside the church. Indeed the way in which he expounds the mysteries and interprets them cannot fail to move his hearers. (45.1-47.2)

Etheria's baptismal account is clear. It is, however, interesting to look at the five stages of this baptismal ceremony, as identified by J. Wilkinson (1981:61-3):

(1) **Registration.** The catechumens who wish to be baptized give in their names before Lent.
(2) **Examination and Enrolment.** The catechumens are examined as to their character and life. If their examiners are satisfied, the catechumens are enrolled and they become accepted candidates for baptism.
(3) **Exorcism and Catechesis.** During the season of Lent the candidates are daily exorcized. They receive a literal and spiritual exposition of the Scriptures and they are also taught the Creed.
(4) **The Baptism.** After the candidates have received their washing at a font elsewhere, they were taken with the bishop to the Anastasis.
(5) **Instruction in the Mysteries.** They are instructed in the meaning of the sacrament which they have received.

It is remarkable to see the similarity between this baptismal account of Etheria and a contemporary description of the celebration of baptism as it is found in the *Mystagogical Lectures* of Cyril of Jerusalem (see chapter 15).

CHAPTER 23

Chrysostom

About 350 John Chrysostom was born of noble Christian parents. He sought a monastic life but he could not fulfil this wish because of the protestations of his widowed mother. Chrysostom therefore led for many years a life of extreme discipline at home, but at the end he spent four years in hermitage. Because of severe illness, he had to return to the church.

In 386 Chrysostom was ordained as a priest. He became famous as a preacher and by reason of his eloquence was called Chrysostom, which means 'golden mouth'. In 398, against his wish, Chrysostom was consecrated bishop of Constantinople. He made many enemies because of his preaching against the depravities of the clergy and the imperial court. Chrysostom was condemned and exiled. When he was forced to travel on foot in severe weather, he died in September 407.

In 1955 A. Wenger discovered a very important manuscript in the monastery of Stavronikita on Mount Athos. It contains a number of baptismal catecheses which were delivered by Chrysostom shortly after 388. These baptismal instructions are of immense value because they shed important light on our understanding of baptism as practised in an important see of the Eastern Church, towards the end of the fourth century A.D. In these catecheses John Chrysostom instructs the baptismal candidates in Christian doctrine and in morality.

The extract from this manuscript which is cited below gives us a clear insight into the baptismal rite in Chrysostom's see:

17. Now let me speak to you about the mysteries themselves and about the contract which will be made between yourselves and the Master. In secular affairs, whenever someone wants to entrust his business to anyone, a written contract must be completed between the trustee and his client. The same thing holds true now, when the Master is entrusting to you not mortal things which are subject to destruction and death, but spiritual things belonging to eternity. Therefore this contract is also called faith since it possesses nothing visible, but only things which can be seen by the eyes of the spirit. There has to be an agreement between the contracting parties. However, this contract is not on paper nor written in ink; it is in God and it is written by the Spirit. The words which you utter here are registered in heaven, and the agreement you make by your tongue remains indelibly with the Master.

18. See here again the external attitude of captivity. The priests bring you in. First they tell you to pray on bent knees, with your hands outstretched to heaven, and to remind yourselves by your posture from what evil you are saved and to what good you will dedicate yourselves. Then the priest comes to you one by one, asks for your contract and confession, and prepares you to utter those terrible and frightening words: 'I renounce you, Satan.'...

20. Then the priest has to say: 'I renounce you, Satan, your pomps, your service, and your works.' The words are few but their power is great. The angels who are standing by and the invisible powers rejoice at your conversion. They receive the words from your tongues, and carry them up to the common Master of all things. There they are inscribed in the books of heaven.

21. Did you see what the terms of the agreement are? After he has renounced the wicked one and all things which are important to him, the priest again has to say:

'And I enter into your service, O Christ.' Did you see His boundless goodness? Receiving only these words from you, He entrusts to you such a store of treasures! He has forgotten all your former unthankfulness, and He reminds you of none of your past deeds, but He is content with these few words.

22. After that contract of renunciation and attachment, after you have confessed His sovereignty and have attached yourself to Christ by the words you spoke, in the next place, as if you were a combatant chosen for the spiritual arena, the priest anoints you on the forehead with the oil of the spirit signing you with the sign of the cross, and says: 'So-and-so is anointed in the name of the Father, and of the Son, and of the Holy Spirit.'

23. The priest knows that henceforth the enemy will be furious and will grind his teeth, going about like a roaring lion when he sees those who were formerly subject to his sovereignty in sudden rebellion against him and that they not only renounce him, but they even go over to the side of Christ. Therefore the priest anoints you on the forehead and signs you with the sign of the cross, in order that the enemy may turn away his eyes. For he does not dare to look you in the face when he sees the lightning flash which leaps forth from your face and blinds his eyes. From that day there is strife and counterstrife with him, and on this account the priest leads you into the spiritual arena as athletes of Christ by virtue of this anointing.

24. Thereafter, in the full darkness of the night, he strips off your robe. Then, as if he were going to lead you into heaven itself by the ritual, he causes your whole body to be anointed with that olive oil of the spirit, so that all your limbs may be fortified and unconquered by the darts aimed at you by the adversary.

25. After this anointing the priest makes you descend into the sacred waters, burying the old man and at the same time raising up the new man, who is renewed in the im-

age of his Creator. At this moment, through the words and the hand of the priest, the Holy Spirit descends upon you. Instead of the man who went down into the water, a different man comes forth, one who has wiped away all the filth of his sins, who has put off the old garment of sin and has put on the royal robe.

26. So that you may also learn from this that the substance of the Father, Son, and Holy Spirit is one, baptism is conferred in the following way: When the priest says: 'So-and-so is baptized in the name of the Father, and of the Son, and of the Holy Spirit,' he puts your head down into the water three times and three times he lifts it up again. By this mystic rite he prepares you to receive the descent of the Spirit. For it is not only the priest who touches the head, but also the right hand of Christ, and this is shown by the very words of the one who baptizes. He does not say: 'I baptize so-and-so,' but: 'So-and-so is baptized,' showing that he is only the minister of grace and that he merely offers his hand because he has been ordained to this end by the Spirit. The one fulfilling all things is the Father and the Son and the Holy Spirit, the undivided Trinity. It is faith in this Trinity which gives the grace of remission from sin; it is this confession which gives to us the gift of filial adoption.

27. What follows shows us from what those, who have been judged worthy of this mystic rite, have been set free, and what they have gained. As soon as they come forth from those sacred waters, all those who are present embrace them, greet them, kiss them, rejoice with them, and congratulate them. Those who were formerly slaves and captives have suddenly become free men and sons and have been invited to the royal table. Immediately thereafter they come up from the waters and they are led to the awesome table, heavy laden with countless favours. There they taste of the Master's body and blood and become a dwelling place for the Holy Spirit. Since they

have put on Christ Himself, wherever they go they are like angels on earth, rivalling the brilliance of the rays of the sun ....

29. Since you stand at the threshold of the royal palace and are about to approach the very throne where sits the King who distributes the gifts, show every ambition in your requests. Only ask for nothing worldly or human; make your petition worthy of Him who grants the gifts. As you come forth from the waters, you symbolize your resurrection by rising up from them. Ask Him to be your ally, so that you may guard well the gifts given to you, and so that you may not be conquered by the deceits of the wicked one. Beg Him for peace among the churches; beseech Him for those who are being led astray; prostrate yourselves on behalf of those who are in sin, so that we may be judged worthy of mercy in some degree. For He has granted you great confidence, He has enrolled you in the front ranks of His friends, and has received into the adoption of sons you who were formerly captives and slaves with no right to speak out. He will not reject your prayers; again imitating in this His own goodness, He will grant you everything you ask. (*Baptismal Catecheses* 2:17-29)

This extract from Chrysostom's *Baptismal Catecheses* highlights the same important features of the baptismal rite as those encountered in other descriptions by contemporary writers. In the first place Chrysostom states in paragraph 17 that *faith* is an important prerequisite for the administration of baptism. In paragraphs 18 and 20 he describes how the baptismal candidate has to *renounce Satan.* This is followed by the *anointment* of the candidate by the priest (see par. 22 and 23). In paragraph 24 Chrysostom, too, testifies about the *laying off of the clothing* of the baptismal candidate. He thereafter gives an explicit description of the administration of baptism by a *threefold immersion.* This is followed by the *kiss* and the *partaking of the eucharist* (see par. 27). The rite of baptism is closed by the *prayers and petitions* of the baptismal candidate. It is clear from paragraph 29 that Chrysostom, too, regarded baptism as a symbol of resurrection.

In the next baptismal catechesis of this same manuscript we read as follows:

> 5. Let us say again: Blessed be God. He alone does wonderful things, and does all things and transforms them. Before yesterday you were captives, but now you are free and citizens of the Church; formerly you lived in the shame of your sins, but now you live in freedom and justice. You are not only free, but also holy; not only holy, but also just; not only just but also sons; not only sons, but also heirs; not only heirs, but also brothers of Christ; not only brothers of Christ, but also joint heirs; not only joint heirs, but also members; not only members, but also the temple; not only the temple, but also instruments of the Spirit.
> 6. Blessed be God. He alone does wonderful things! You have seen how numerous are the gifts of baptism. Although many men believe that the only gift baptism confers is the remission of sins, we have counted its honours to the number of ten. It is on this account that we baptize even children although they are sinless, that they may be given the further gifts of sanctification, justice, filial adoption, and inheritance, that they may be brothers and members of Christ, and become dwelling places for the Spirit. (*Baptismal Catecheses* 3:5-6)

In the extract above Chrysostom elaborates on the performative function of baptism (i.e. that baptism does something to a person) when he enumerates all the gifts bestowed by the administration of baptism. He names ten benefits. It is very interesting that Chrysostom argues that baptism is administered to children so that they can partake of these benefits. Note the total lack of the covenant idea in his motivation for child baptism. Neither did Chrysostom believe in original sin since he declares these children as 'sinless'. This explains why Chrysostom does not include the 'remission of sins' in the list of benefits bestowed by baptism. Infants who are sinless do not need the remission of sins!

This passage from Chrysostom's writings is very interesting, since it gives us an insight into the theology underlying the baptism as practised by the Church Fathers. It also makes clear that the belief in the performative function of baptism (i.e. that baptism does something to a person) facilitated the transition to the practice of infant baptism, since the ten benefits were also conferred upon children who are explicitly designated as 'sinless'. This qualification suggests that the children were possibly very small. Chrysostom refers to these by the Greek word παῖδες. As we have already seen in chapter 9 this Greek term referred to children including younger and older children. How young these 'sinless' children were is not clear, since the baptismal rite as described by Chrysostom could easily have been administered to young children, but hardly to helpless infants. Nowhere in Chrysostom, or any other writer for that matter, can one find any indication of a different rite specifically for babies. Since we have seen in chapters 1 and 8 that guardians were indeed involved to answer the questions put to little children who were not able to respond for themselves, one may conclude that in the time of Chrysostom the general rite, as performed in the case of adults, was also extended to children and even possibly very young ones. This shows how incorrect it would be to think that infant baptism came to be practised at a particular point in time. No, it was a matter of the usual rite of baptism upon confession of belief gradually being extended to very young children. At a time when sporadic instances of infant baptism can be recognized, it is understandable that the fourth century can legitimately be seen as a transition towards the later general custom of infant baptism.

CHAPTER 24

Theodore of Mopsuestia

Theodore was born about the year 350. He studied rhetoric under the famous pagan Libanius, but afterwards under Diodore of Tarsus, the great Christian teacher. While he was a student at the school of the sophist Libanius, he met Chrysostom and their friendship lasted throughout their lives. In 392 Theodore was consecrated bishop of Mopsuestia in Cilicia. He died in A.D. 428.

Theodore was a prolific author but many of his writings are extant only in a multitude of fragments. Fortunately Oriental versions of some of these works have been discovered. One such work is Theodore's *Catechetical Homilies* which were known only from a few isolated fragments. The Syriac text was discovered by A. Mingana who published it in 1932. These homilies were delivered by Theodore most probably between 388-92 (Quasten 1975:1.409). There are sixteen catecheses and numbers 12-14 give us a very interesting picture of the baptismal liturgy as practised towards the end of the fourth century. The following excerpts are from Theodore's introductions to each of the three catecheses dealing with baptism.

In his introduction to homily nr. 12 Theodore writes as follows:

> He who desires to come to the gift of the holy baptism, comes to the Church of God where he is received by a duly appointed person (there is a habit to register those who draw nigh unto baptism) who will question him

about his way of life. This rite is performed in the case of those who are baptized by a person called 'guardian'. The duly appointed person writes your name in the Church register together with the name of the one who is acting as your sponsor or guide in the town. The ministries of the persons called exorcists are also indispensable, as it is necessary that when a case is being heard in the judgment hall, the litigant should remain silent. You stand with outstretched arms in the posture of one who prays, and you look downwards. This is the reason why you take off your outer garment and stand barefooted. You stand also on sackcloth. You are ordered in those days to meditate on the words of the faith. (*Homily* XII *Prol.*)

Note that Theodore says that the way of life of the baptismal candidate has to be scrutinized before he is accepted for baptism. Thereafter the candidate took off his outer garment, denounced Satan and confessed his belief in Jesus Christ, according to the prologue of the thirteenth homily:

You stand barefooted on sackcloth while your outer garment is taken off from you and your hands are stretched towards God in the posture of the one who prays. First you bend your knees while the rest of your body is upright, and then you say: 'I denounce Satan and all his angels, and all his works, and all his service, and all his deception, and all his worldly glory; I commit myself and believe, and I am baptized in the name of the Father, and of the Son, and of the Holy Spirit.' While you are bending your knees, and the rest of your body is upright, and your look is directed towards heaven, and your hands are outstretched in the posture of one who prays, the priest, clad in clean and shining linen robes, signs you on your forehead with the Holy Anointment and says: 'So-and-so is signed in the name of the Father, and of the Son and of the Holy Spirit.' And your godfather who is standing behind you spreads a linen cloth on the crown of your head, raises you and makes you stand upright. (*Homily* XIII, *Prol.*)

In the prologue to the next homily, Theodore gives us an explicit description of the baptism of an adult person by means of immersion:

> You come to the holy baptism, and first take off all your clothing, after which you are properly and thoroughly anointed with holy Chrism. The priest begins and says: 'So-and-so is anointed in the name of the Father, and of the Son and of the Holy Spirit.' Then you go down into the water that has been consecrated by the blessing of the priest, who, dressed as described above, stands up and stretches out his hand, which he places on your head and says: 'So-and-so is baptized in the name of the Father, and of the Son, and of the Holy Spirit.' He places his hand on your head and says, 'in the name of the Father,' and with these words he immerses in the water. If you were allowed to speak there you would have said 'Amen!', but you simply plunge into the water and incline your head downwards; and the priest says 'and of the Son', and with his hand immerses you again while you also incline your head downwards; and the priest says 'and of the Holy Spirit', and presses you down and immerses you again in a similar way. After you have left that place, you put on a very radiant garment, and the priest comes and signs you on your forehead and says: 'So-and-so is signed in the name of the Father, and of the Son, and of the Holy Spirit.' (*Homily* XIV, *Prol.*)

Theodore's description of the administration of baptism corresponds largely with the account given by other Church Fathers of the fourth century.

CHAPTER 25

Early Christian art

In all the previous chapters our conclusions are based on what the early Christians *wrote* about practices in their own times. However, another important source of information is the *art* of the early Christians. Modern scholars often appeal to catacomb art to 'prove' that sprinkling was the mode of baptism in the early church (cf. Barnard 1984:86; Du Preez 1985:6-9; Floor 1983:54; Kerr 1944:79; Oetting 1970:29; Walker 1970:88). They then usually refer to depictions such as the following:

Fig. 1: A wall-painting in the catacomb of Calixtus. Third century.

Early Christian art 173

Fig. 2: The baptism of Christ. Late third century.
Catacomb of Saint Peter and Saint Marcellinus, Rome.

Fig. 3: The baptism of Christ.
Sarcophagus, Rome. Santa Maria antique.

These scholars then draw attention to the boyhood of the baptismal candidate, the affusion of the water and the fact that the water is merely ankle deep. Du Preez (1985:7), who defends the sprinkling of babies, says that these pictures do tell us about the mode of baptism as practised in the time of the artist. Möller, on the other hand, wants to play down the 'testimony' of these pictures because it does not suit his own theological beliefs. Möller therefore says: 'The fact that pictures of sprinkling in the first century are found in the subterranean catacomb in Rome, means nothing. It cannot be proved that these pictures were painted in the first century.'[1] But the *dating* of these pictures is not the question at issue. Moreover, a large number of these pictures undoubtedly date from the second and third century. Thus these pictures nevertheless bear testimony to a very early period of the church and need to be taken into consideration. Let us therefore consider this important source.

In the first place one should remember that, just as a written text, art can also lead to erroneous conclusions if it is interpreted at face value. This often happens in the case of early Christian art. One of the serious mistakes which scholars make is that they do not always take into consideration the symbolic nature of early Christian art. Early Christian art was not a pictorial representation of the reality. It was never the intention of the artist to portray an actual scene, but rather to convey its notion or meaning. This very important aspect of early Christian art becomes clear when we look at how the early Christian artists portrayed popular biblical scenes. Let us take the portrayal of Noah and the ark as an example:

---

[1] The original Afrikaans version reads:
   Die feit dat in die onderaardse katakombes te Rome prente is van die besprinkeling in die eerste eeu, sê nog niks. Dit kan nie bewys word dat daardie prente in die eerste eeu geskilder is nie (Möller 1976:201).

Early Christian art 175

Fig. 4: Noah in the ark. Third century.
Catacomb of Saint Peter and Saint Marcellinus, Rome.

There are more than forty depictions of Noah in the ark in catacomb art, dating from the second till the end of the fourth century. All these depictions of Noah are very similar: The ark is always a square box. Noah is depicted standing upright in this boxlike ark, in a position of prayer, with his arms outstretched. Usually there is also a dove, bearing an olive branch in its beak or in its claws, and it is portrayed as flying towards Noah. It is very interesting that in none of these scenes are any animals present. Neither is the ark depicted as a three-storey boat. The reason for this is that the artist did not want to depict every detail of the story of Noah. He only wanted to convey the meaning which the story of Noah and the ark had for him. The saving of Noah from the flood was probably seen as a type of salvation of a believer through baptism, as in 1 Peter 3:20-21.

Similarly in the depictions of baptismal scenes the artist is merely portraying all the persons and elements that were present at a baptismal ceremony, namely the one who baptizes, the one who is being baptized, the water and the dove. (The dove is a symbol of the Holy Spirit, which was conferred on a believer at his baptism, according to some Church Fathers.)

Thus these pictures do not in any respect bear testimony to the mode of baptism at the time of the artist, as is often claimed in modern works. If one insists on interpreting the water pouring over the baptismal candidate as evidence for sprinkling, one should likewise conclude that the early Christians administered baptism with water coming from the beak of a dove (see figure 2). This surely shows that it is incorrect to interpret early Christian art as an exact representation of the reality.

But how should we explain the relative smallness of the baptismal candidate in the baptismal scenes (figures 1-3)? It was common practice among the early Christians to depict a benefactor as much larger in size than the recipient. Thus when the artists depicted Jesus as healer, he was always much larger in size than those who experienced his healing. Let us look, for example, at figure 5:

Early Christian art 177

Fig. 5: The healing of the paralytic and of the man born blind.
Sarcophagus, Lateran museum, Rome.

In figure 5 Jesus heals the paralytic and the blind man. Note the relative smallness of the paralytic and the blind man (i.e. the recipients) compared to the size of Jesus (i.e. the benefactor). Likewise, in figures 1-3 the person who baptizes is seen as the benefactor while the baptismal candidate is seen as the recipient and this explains the relative smallness of the latter.

On the other hand, one should not think that there is no relation whatsoever between scenes in early Christian art and reality. The key is that conclusions drawn from writings and from art should supplement and not contradict each other. It is important to realize that written documents and art fulfil the same function since both serve as a means of communication. Thus when somebody wishes to say something, he has various means by which he may express himself. Writing and art are two of those means. Thus it is unlikely that written documents and pieces of art, originating from the same place and period of time, would give contradictory accounts of the world in which they came into being. To interpret the baptismal scenes above as bearing testimony to the practice of sprinkling and of infant baptism in the church of the first four centuries, would go directly against all the explicit descriptions which we encountered in the writings of the Church Fathers and which we discussed in the previous chapters.

Let us now study the following baptismal scene dating from the second/third century:

Fig. 6: Tomb of Lucian, Second to third century.

In this picture we once again see that the baptismal candidate is much smaller in size than the person who baptizes. The reasons are the same as given above. But note also that the candidate is naked while the person who administers the baptism is clothed. We did read in many of the writings quoted in the previous chapters that the baptismal candidates took off their clothing as a symbol of the laying off of the old life. Thus actual details of the customs are also reflected in the pictorial art of the early Christians. It is important to realize that pictorial art should be examined in conjunction with explicit verbal descriptions in the related literature, before a painting or sculpture can be analyzed and appreciated.

CHAPTER 26

Conclusions

Baptism as such is not a rite peculiar to Christianity. Many other religions of the ancient world practised baptism as an initiation rite. The notion of washing, which is such an obvious aspect of baptism, provided the essence of purifying a person in order for that person to be accepted into a particular religious community. Irenaeus, especially, referred to how Christian baptism, which in a way also entails initiation into the circle of believers, differs substantially from the similar rites in other religions, since Christian baptism is not so much an act of initiation, as it is a sign of regeneration. The person baptized becomes a new person. The old life permeated by sin is cleansed. Therefore remission or washing away of sins played a central role in the rite of Christian baptism throughout the early stages of the Christian church. The notion of regeneration provided a symbolic feature while remission of sins involved a performative act (that is, an act which does something to the recipient). The event of baptism bestows upon the person certain benefits. Thus, Christian baptism in its earlier stages was explained, and practised, with major or minor emphasis on these basic notions.

The oldest writings emphasized these basic notions by focusing on the relevance of water and the cross of Christ, as can already be seen in the Epistle of Barnabas. Going down into the baptismal water symbolized participation in the death of Christ on the cross and performed, at the same time, a washing away of sins, so that the person emerging from the water is performatively cleansed and regenerated symbolically, by sharing in the death and resurrection of Christ. The theology underlying these conceptions was linked to Paul's statement in Romans 6 that baptism entails being baptized into the death of Christ. Even in the fourth century we still find a number of significant expositions of baptism linked closely to dying with Christ and being raised up with Him into a new life. Therefore, fasting, prayer and instruction played a dominant role in preparing a person for receiving baptism. Justin's remarks are very clear. Baptism requires a declared belief in the teachings of Christ, a life substantiating this belief, and partaking of the eucharist, that is, sharing in Christ's atonement on the cross. Remission of sin was intimately linked with God's forgiveness entreated by prayer and fasting. Regeneration, involving dying with Christ and being raised up with Christ into a new life, was the most central notion associated with Christian baptism. In later full and lengthy descriptions of the actual rite as preserved, for example, in the writings of Cyril, Basil, Ambrose, Etheria, Chrysostom and Theodore in the fourth century, regeneration was also symbolized by the removal of clothes when entering the baptismal water and thus descending naked into the font as if to completely part with one's old life. This act was then followed by the candidate's ascension from the water, as if he were a new creature; this would be further symbolized by his receiving new clothes (often white clothes). Some writers, such as Tertullian, Hippolytus and Cyril, also relate how exorcism, anointing with oil and laying on of hands accompanied the baptismal event, in order to denounce the devil and to partake of the Holy Spirit.

Within the practice of baptism in the early church these symbolic features underscored the original, theological base, at least in the first three centuries. However, one should never think of the early church as a unity having a specific codified dogma. The first four centuries is a compendium of various points of view and various emphases on many issues. While in one area of the ancient world a particular view prevailed, other theologies were developing and became dominant in other areas. This can be seen best in the development of infant baptism which was already strongly advocated and practised in North Africa in the third century while the same occurred much later, during the latter part of the fourth century, in Europe and Asia.

The theory and practice of baptism in the first four centuries of the Christian faith hovered between the basic notions of symbol and performance as explained at the beginning of this chapter. The performative function of baptism, however, was responsible for a gradual development away from its being construed as occasioning remission of sins to its being a rite which was seen (especially in the views expounded by Chrysostom) as conferring a large number of benefits on the recipient. Baptism as a performative rite emphasized sacramental issues, in that baptism was seen within this frame of reference as a rite administered and controlled, as it were, by the church. Note, for example, how Cyprian insisted that a person should 'be baptized and sanctified in the Catholic Church, with the lawful, and true and only baptism of the Church' (cf. p. 95). The Church, as custodian of the rite of baptism, thereby grants benefits to the receivers of baptism. The mere act of baptism was seen as a guarantee of mainly three benefits bestowed upon the recipient. Some of our authors would combine two or more of these, while others would emphasize a particular performative act. These three benefits were that baptism effects (1) remission of sins, (2) guaranteed entrance into the Kingdom of heaven, that is, it ensures salvation, and (3) bestowal of a number of spiritual blessings. Chrysostom lists ten such blessings besides remission of sins, such as filial adoption, sanctification and the indwelling of the Holy Spirit.

It is important to recognize that the view of baptism as performative entailed a quite distinct theological presupposition from that underlying the symbolic view. This also shows how misleading it is to think of the so-called early church as operating in terms of one theological perspective. The performative perspective allowed for various developments. The contention that a person receives forgiveness of sins by the very rite of baptism provided occasion for the question as to when to administer baptism. In some areas church leaders advocated a postponement of baptism, preferably as close to death as possible. The rationale was that after baptism a person could not sin again, since one is then supposed to enter heaven in a properly purified state. Others deemed that since baptism guarantees entrance to the heavenly world, it is too much of a risk to postpone baptism. One never knows when some misfortune may occur thus leaving the person to die unbaptized. But what then of remission of sins? Some argued that baptism administered at an early age would be sufficient to cover all future sin - a real safeguard. Others, especially during the third and fourth centuries when the doctrine of inherited original sin began to develop, reasoned that baptism sets one free from the taint of sin which clings to a person entering the world. This entailed two points of view. Some argued for an early baptism though not forgetting that the actual rite required certain confessions and enactments. These proponents advocated an age of three years at least in order for the person receiving baptism to be aware of what is happening. Others linked baptism by analogy to circumcision. These either required baptism to be performed on the eighth day after birth, or preferably earlier since the delay may be dangerous in view of the contention that if such a person should die unbaptized there is no hope of salvation and eternal life. Therefore, whenever a person fell seriously ill, irrespective of age, such a person was immediately baptized as a precaution. This type of baptism is often referred to in modern writings as clinical baptism or emergency baptism.

In the first four centuries of Christianity, the literature on baptism clearly shows how, in the majority of instances, it was persons of responsible age (generally adults and grown children) who were recipients of baptism. Emergency baptism and the eventual linking of baptism to circumcision, as well as the fact that baptism was believed to remove sin, occasioned the extension of baptism to small children and finally to infants. Though some authors (Tertullian and Gregory of Nazianzus) opposed this development, others (Cyprian) strongly advocated this trend, contending that no one is to be deprived of salvation and all the gifts of God's grace. Within this theological framework, baptism became (especially in the way it is formulated by Chrysostom) the most exclusive donator of Christian blessings. The symbol became the actual means. The rite of baptism itself, rather than Christ, became the guarantee of eternal salvation.

The patristic literature of the first four centuries clearly shows how infant baptism developed. Probably the first instances known, occurred in the latter part of the third century, mostly in North Africa, but during the fourth century infant baptism became more and more accepted and though believer's baptism of people of responsible age still continued in many areas, the development of the church (after church and State became reconciled) into a more unified body, controlled by the see of Rome, provided a theological base for infant baptism to be accepted. While the third century voiced objections against what appears to have been a growth in the number of infants being baptized, the fourth century seems to have accepted these baptisms along with adult baptism which was still performed on a regular scale. It may, however, be said that since the fourth century infant baptism began to develop into a generally accepted custom.

It would also be wrong to assume that adults were baptized up to a certain point in time, and that infant baptism was then instituted. The patristic literature discussed in this book represents data, clearly showing that the age of a person as such was not an issue. It was a matter of confessing personal belief, and understanding what baptism meant. Children (but not infants), were often baptized, also within the framework of the symbolic signification of baptism. Infant baptism began to be practised mainly as a result of the performative function associated with baptism, wherever the significance of this function was pressed to its limits as, for example, by Cyprian and Chrysostom. It is, therefore, also extremely important to note that the performative function of baptism was applied to the baptism of every person, not only young children and infants. It is merely that this view of the significance of baptism allowed for infants to be baptized.

The history of the rite of Christian baptism in the first four centuries of Christianity is essentially tied to theological perspectives on the basic significance of baptism - what it is and what it does. This also explains why the method of administering baptism was never an issue. It is true that the 'sprinkling' (in fact, affusion) of the person to be baptized, as in the case of clinical or emergency baptism of seriously ill people, was at times contested, as is known from the case of Novatian and in comments made by Cyprian. However, while immersion seems to have been the regular practice, the mode was never a real issue. It is the *meaning* of baptism that underscored the different theologies and practices. When 'sprinkling' was administered it involved a proper wetting and not a few drops on the forehead. One should be cautious not to transpose the meaning of present day terms (such as sprinkling, for example) into the practices of the ancient world without first ascertaining what was actually involved. Yet, on the other hand, it can be legitimately concluded from our literature that the actual method was not much of an issue as already stated in the *Didache*.

It is also remarkable that the link between baptism and circumcision became relevant only when the issue of the age of the one to be baptized became crucial. And even then one should not assume that the third and fourth centuries saw a fully developed doctrine of baptism replacing circumcision. It was more a matter of analogy than dogma. This also explains why the Abrahamic covenant is hardly ever mentioned. These aspects belong to a later stage of development for which the theologies of the fourth century laid the foundation.

Finally, it needs to be remarked that the contention often found in modern literature, viz. that adult baptism in the early church entailed a missionary situation, cannot be substantiated by the relevant patristic literature, since the transition from adult baptism to infant baptism occurred at a time when Christianity was already a widespread phenomenon in the ancient church. Therefore, it is also unsound to scrutinize the New Testament writings for allusions to infant baptism, since the latter involved a historical development. Moreover, no distinction was ever made between persons coming from a heathen or Christian family. In fact, the reason for the transition to infant baptism was one of theological perspective and had nothing to do with a missionary situation.

The patristic sources are valuable witnesses in supplying the setting in which the teachings of the New Testament writings found their way not only into the lives of the early Christians as individuals, but also into the life and society of the ancient world from which our modern world developed. As such these sources provide crucial data for understanding the world we live in.

Bibliography

Aland, K. *Did the Early Church baptize infants?* The Westminster Press (Philadelphia, 1963)
(Translated from the German by G.R. Beasly-Murray, *Die Säuglingstaufe im Neuen Testament und in der Alten Kirche: Eine Antwort an Joachim Jeremias.*) Chr. Kaiser Verlag, (München, 1961)

Ancient. *Ancient Christian writers* (ed. by J. Quasten *et alii.*) (1946ff)

Ante-Nicene. *The Ante-Nicene Father.* (American ed.) Wm.B. Eerdmans Publishing Co. (Grand Rapids, 1884ff)

Barnard, A.C. *Ek is gedoop,* N.G. Kerkboekhandel (Pretoria, 1984)

Bridge, D. & Phypers, D. *The water that divides,* Inter-Varsity Press, (England, 1977)

Connolly, R.H. *Didascalia Apostolorum,* (the Syriac version translated and accompanied by the Verona Latin Fragments) Clarendon Press (Oxford, 1929)

Cross, F.L. *The Early Christian Fathers,* Gerald Duckworth & Co. Ltd, (London, 1960)

Cuming, G.J. *Hippolytus: A text for students,* (with introduction, translation, commentary and notes) Grove Books (Bramcote Notts, 1976)

De Beus, C. *De Oud-Christelijke doop en zijn voorgeschiedenis,* Vol. 2. Tjeenk Willink. (Haarlem, 1948)

Di Berardino, A. *Patrology,* Vol. 4. Christian Classics, Inc. (Westminster, 1986)

Didier, J.C. Le pédobaptisme au IVe siècle. Documents nouveaux. *Mélanges de Science Religieuse (6),* 233-246 (1949)

Didier, J.C. *Le baptême des enfants dans la tradition de l'église,* Monumenta Christiana Selecta VII (Tournai, 1959)

Diehl, E. *Inscriptiones Latinae Christianae Veteres,* (Berlin, 1961)

Du Preez, J. *Besprenkeling as doopvorm? ('n Studie oor die modus van die sakrament van die Christelike doop),* Vol. 7, Reeks B, Nr. 1, Annale (Universiteit van Stellenbosch, 1985)

Easton, B.S. *The Apostolic tradition of Hippolytus,* (translated into English with introduction and notes) Cambridge University Press (Cambridge, 1934)

Engelbrecht, J.J. Verbond en kinderdoop in die patristiese literatuur - enkele opmerkings. *Hervormde Teologiese Tydskrif,* Jg. 40, Afl. 3, 56-61 (1984)

Fathers. *The Fathers of the Church,* Catholic University Press, Inc (Washington, 1947ff).

Ferguson, E. Inscriptions and the origin of infant baptism, *Journal of Theological Studies,* Vol. 30, 37-46. (1979)

Floor, L. 1983. *Die Heilige Doop in die Nuwe Testament,* Potchefstroomse Teologiese Publikasie (Noordbrug, 1983)

Hermans, J. *Herboren uit water en Heilige Geest,* Tabor (Brugge, 1983)

Jeremias, J. *Infant baptism in the first four centuries,* SCM Press (London, 1960)
(Translated from the German by D. Cairns, *Die Kindertaufe in den ersten vier Jahrhunderten,* Vandenhoeck and Ruprecht (Göttingen, 1958)

Kerr, H.T. *The Christian sacraments. A source book for ministers,* The Westminster Press (Philadelphia, 1944)

König, A, Lederle, H.I. & Möller, F.P. *Infant baptism? The arguments for and against,* (Proceedings of a theological congress held at University of South Africa, 3-5 October 1983) Cum Books (Roodepoort, 1984)

Kraft, H. *Texte zur Geschichte der Taufe, besonders der Kindertaufe in der alten Kirche,* Verlag Walter de Gruyter & Co. (Berlin, 1969)

Lewis, J.P. Baptismal practices of the second and third century church, *Restoration Quarterly,* Vol. 26, Nr. 1, 1-17 (1983)

Liddell, H.G. & Scott, R. *Greek-English Lexicon,* Clarendon Press (Oxford, 1961)

Loeb. *Loeb Classical Library,* Harvard University Press (Cambridge, 1912ff)

Luik, A.G. *Baptisterium,* J.H. Kok (Kampen, 1975)

Marais, W. *Die kinderdoop en besprinkeling. Ja of nee?* W & M Uitgewers (Pretoria, 1974)

Migne, J.P. *Patrologiae Cursus Completus,* (Paris, 1884ff)

Mingana, A. *Woodbrooke studies,* Vol. 6. (Christian documents edited and translated with a critical apparatus) W. Heffer & Sons Ltd. (Cambridge, 1933)

Möller, F.P. *Die sakrament in gedrang.* Die Evangelie Uitgewers (Braamfontein, 1976)

New International. *The New International Dictionary of the Christian Church,* Paternoster Press (Great Britain, 1974)

Nicene. *The Nicene and Post-Nicene Father,* First and second series, (American ed.) Wm. B. Eerdmans Publishing Co. (Grand Rapids, 1886ff)

Oetting, W. *The church of the catacombs.* Concordia Publishing House (Saint Louis, 1970)

Oxford Dictionary. *The Oxford Dictionary of the Christian Church,* (ed. by F.L. Cross) Oxford University Press (Oxford, 1978 (1957)

Pretorius, N.F. *Die Didaché Die onderwysing van die Twaalf Apostels,* N.G. Kerk Uitgewers (Pretoria, 1980)

Quasten, J. *Patrology,* Vols. 1-3, Spectrum Publishers (Utrecht, 1975, 1953)

Sources. *Sources Chrétiennes* (Paris, 1941ff)

Stander, H.F. Baptism and the interpretation of early Christian art, *Hervormde Teologiese Studies*, Vol. 43, 316-324 (1987)

Story, C.I.K. Justin's apology I.62-64: Its importance for the author's treatment of Christian baptism, *Vigiliae Christianae*, Vol. 16, 172-178 (1962)

Torrance, T.F. The origins of baptism, *Scottish Journal of Theology*, Vol. 11, 158-171 (1958)

Van den Berg, L.J.C. *Die doop en charismata: Die leer van die Pinkster Protestante Kerk krities beskou.* (Unpublished BD thesis, 1981)

Vokes, F.E. *The riddle of the Didache,* The Macmillan Co. (New York, 1938)

Vööbus, A. *Liturgical traditions in the Didache,* Etse (Stockholm, 1968)

Walker, W. *A history of the Christian Church,* T & T Clark (Edinburgh,1970)

Wand, J.W.C. *A history of the Early Church to A.D. 500,* Methuen & Co. Ltd (London, 1949 (1937).

Westminster Dictionary. *The Westminster Dictionary of Church History,* The Westminster Press (Philadelphia, 1971)

Wilkinson, J. *Egeria's travels to the Holy Land,* (Revised ed.) Aris & Phillips (Warminster, 1981)

Wood, S. *Fathers of the Church: Christ the Educator,* Catholic University of America Press (Washington, 1954)

Zwi Werblowsky, R.J. On the baptismal rite according to St. Hippolytus. *Studia Patristica*, Vol. 2. (Ed. by K. Aland and F.L. Cross) Akademie Verlag (Berlin, 1957)